design & make
hats

KAREN HENRIKSEN

WITH PHOTOGRAPHY BY SUSSIE AHLBURG

DISCLAIMER

Everything written in this book is to the best of my knowledge true and every effort has been made to ensure accuracy and safety, but neither author nor publisher can be held responsible for any resulting injury, damage or loss to either persons or property. Any further information which will assist in updating of any future editions would be gratefully received. Read through all the information in each chapter before commencing work. Follow all health and safety guidelines and where necessary obtain health and safety information from the suppliers.

All hats, except where stated, by Karen Henriksen.
All photography, except where stated, by Sussie Ahlburg.

First published in Great Britain 2008
A&C Black Publishers
36 Soho Square
London W1D 3QY
www.acblack.com

ISBN 978-0-7136-8738-5

Frontispiece: Classic Straw Hat by Karen Henriksen

Book design: Susan McIntyre and Sutchinda Thompson
Cover design: Sutchinda Thompson
Commissioning editor: Susan James
Managing Editor: Sophie Page
Copy editor: Jo Waters
Proof reader: Julian Beecroft

Printed and bound in China

Contents

ACKNOWLEDGEMENTS

Many thanks to Sussie Ahlburg for sharing and realising my ideas
for beautiful and inspirational as well as informative photography.
My gratitude also to the models for bringing the hats to life with
such style, energy and verve: Pietra Mello-Pittman, Janine Jauvel,
Jennifer Chapman, Kirsty Parsons and James Frayne.
Thank you to the editors and designers for their enthusiasm,
patience and dilligence, and to my fellow hard-working milliners for
allowing their work to be included here.
Finally, thank you to John for his constant support and his
appreciation that writing about hats is as time-consuming and
all-absorbing as designing and making them.

introduction

Of all fashion accessories, hats are the most personal and the most powerful. How could they fail to be, worn as they are on the most important, the most visible and the most photographed part of the body? Hats frame the face, and make one walk tall; they cause heads to turn, and compliments to follow. They can be used to project or to shield. Hats are also signifiers, immediately evocative of a particular era, or movement, or mood. They can provide a shorthand, helping to place a look, where other garments might be too heavy-handed, too fancy dress.

Yet, people so often say that although they love them, hats don't suit them personally, or else they don't have the confidence to wear them. In reality, of course, hats give you confidence. And, as any milliner will assure you, there is a hat for everyone. But, if you have picked up this book, then perhaps you already know this?

Any discussion about hats so often becomes a discussion about why we don't wear hats anymore. By hats, this should perhaps be qualified to mean the more formal, blocked type of hat. Certainly the busier and more crowded (literally, at rush hour) lifestyles we lead are a key factor, but we have also become more casual and less deferential in our culture generally. This change has of course been gradual; the trauma of two world wars had at least as much to do with this as the swinging '60s, which is generally acknowledged as the final blow for the hat. With their history so bound up with status, etiquette, religion and generally 'knowing one's place', hats inevitably had a hard time of it. And a hard time it certainly was, with the industry decimated particularly through the 1960s and '70s. During the 1980s and '90s, although the industry remained in decline, at least there was a return to fashion for hats, with power dressing, the 'Lady Diana effect', and such notable milliners as Stephen Jones and Philip Treacy emerging, each with their own style. The more vibrant and hat-friendly music scenes also helped: hats have always been the perfect tool for striking a pose, projecting an image, for displaying attitude.

Since then, in this age of pluralism, the general trend has been towards a softer, easier and very casual style of dress. In response, casual hats for both men and women have seen an upsurge; the arrival and growth of street culture and sportswear and their acceptance into the mainstream has had a major impact on casual headwear, perhaps men's in particular. Occasion wear has also moved towards a more relaxed style of dress, accessorised by creations which perch on the side of the head – variously known as 'fascinators', cocktail hats or headpieces.

The UK, with its tradition of the 'season', saw less of a decline in formal headwear than anywhere else; hats have continued to be worn for public events such as Royal Ascot, as well as for weddings and other private occasions, despite the vagaries of fashion trends. Elsewhere in the world, hat traditions have perhaps placed more emphasis on protection than occasion. And while the very British notion of dressing up and hat-wearing has been exported around the world, there has been a returned favour, with more and more people in Britain wearing fashionable, stylish hats for protection from the elements as much as for show. Indeed, today with our more exacting standards, it is not enough for a hat simply to be functional and practical – we rightly also demand that it be stylish and fashionable.

Recent times have seen something of a paradox happening: clothes and accessories in the mass market are cheaper and more disposable than ever; yet at the same time there has also been a major trend for vintage pieces and thrift-shop finds, and alongside this has been a revival in the appreciation of handmade and bespoke. Perhaps this is a reaction against the universal casual blandness of the high street and towards a desire to infuse an element of glamour or luxury into modern dress, and it is the hat more than any other item of clothing that can do this to such great effect.

While dressing for an occasion or for protection are still the leading motivations behind most decisions to wear a hat, there are also times when a hat is worn 'just because'. And the more milliners producing hats that are innovative, desirable and relevant, the more this will continue to happen. For many years we have no longer been obliged to put on a hat everyday, but perhaps we will see a revival in people choosing to wear one 'just because'.

This exotic gold headpiece by Edwina Ibbotson has a metallic leather base, with striking use of ostrich quill, diamante encrusted spines and sharply cut turkey feathers. The effect is softened by a fitted face veil, also with scattered crystals. PHOTO: JOANNE ALDRIDGE

TOP A modern trilby style hat in vibrant pink velour felt by Misa Harada; the two delicate butterflies appear to have just landed on the crown, adding a light and witty note to a winter hat.
PHOTO: DAISUKE HONDA

ABOVE This headpiece is made using gold metallic lambskin over a buckram base, and is complemented by the vintage paper braid that has been arranged into a spiraling flower. From Rustic Luxe couture collection

A perching visor in parasisal straw, with a crin-covered quill as a
light yet dramatic trim. From Up Up & Away couture collection.

1 design & inspiration

In many ways, of course, design is very personal and a matter of taste. But there are general principles and rules which are broadly acknowledged. Of course, rules are there to be broken, but as with any design discipline it's a good idea to really grasp these principles before attempting to break them!

Generally, trimmings on hats should follow the line of the hat itself, so if a brim slopes down on the right, then the trimming would be positioned to the right. Trimmings tend to be the most successful when there is a lightness of touch, as though they have just fallen into place, but as is so often the case, something which looks effortless can be the most difficult thing to achieve! I believe this to be true of more avant-garde designs as much as with traditional hats.

This collection of mood boards, design drawings and fabric swatches relates to research into hairstyles across several eras, as well as a more in-depth look at fashion icons from the 1940s onwards.

RIGHT Varnished Japanese paper visor with silk satin organza 'cloud', from Suffragette City couture collection. For this collection I was interested in the immense volume and heavy use of feathers of the hats worn in the Edwardian period, at the height of the Suffragette movement, but wanted to create modern hats that were light and minimalist – rather contrasting aesthetics!

I find that inspiration can come from many varied sources. It can be architecture, sculpture, a painting or simply a word or a phrase, or often a combination of contrasting elements. I might often have an historic, romantic or extravagant element alongside a contrasting, perhaps more modern, theme, which pulls the designs into a more contemporary look and feel than might otherwise be the case. For example, an extravagant cloud of wispy organza might sit on a sharp visor shape, preventing it becoming too frothy or girly. Mixing leather with straw can offer a slightly unexpected twist, as can vintage finds used with modern shapes or fabrics.

Most designers will keep notebooks or sketchbooks containing ideas and drawings alongside fabric swatches, photographs, cuttings, etc. A typical fashion/textile designer's, or indeed milliner's, notebook is likely to be impossible to close!

It is important not to let your theme, or inspiration, get in the way of a good hat! Inspiration should be just that – a starting point from which to explore. If you find yourself veering off in an entirely different direction, it's usually best to go with the flow. The resulting hat is likely to be a more successful design than when rigidly trying to make a hat fit in with a particular theme if it doesn't want to go there. Not only does it free up the thinking and design process, but you are more likely to find your own 'voice'.

Shape is very important in my own designs, possibly before anything else. Designing and making are for me an integrated process, something I feel is in common with most other milliners. While fashion designers' work might sometimes be carried out by draping on the stand, garment design generally is much more of a two-dimensional design process. Certainly with model (couture) millinery, the individual signature of the milliner is not only seen in the design of the hat, but is found in literally every stitch, cut and drape of the hat itself. In this sense, millinery could be seen as a relatively accessible form of couture – while model hats are expensive, they are not often in the same league as couture clothing.

Once the basics have been grasped, it can be rewarding to create your own shapes, sometimes taking elements from existing, more generic-shaped blocks, or from your own patterns. These can then either become a base for a one-off fabric-covered hat, or remain as toiles, or prototypes, with the same treatment being applied to a straw or felt. Mannequin or 'dolly' heads are useful when developing a new shape. These are now quite difficult to source, although most block-makers do make wooden head-shaped blocks, which are also useful for blocking over when a head-piece needs to fit the head perfectly. An inexpensive polystyrene display head can be used if there is no dolly head available, but be aware that the head size on display heads is very small indeed, so these should only be used as a stand, rather than for any precise measuring. But in any case it is even better to keep checking the effect on your own head – a mirror is probably a more vital piece of equipment even than a mannequin head! And of course it is important to see how the hat looks from all angles.

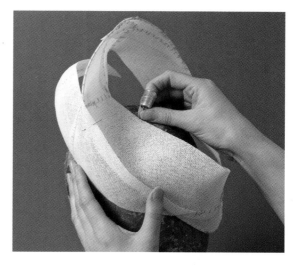

Pinning together two brim shapes to create a new hat shape.

When working on more abstract ideas for shape, it might seem obvious, but make sure that you are actually designing a hat, rather than a piece of sculpture that is somehow going to be worn on the head! There is a difference, one which is perhaps the essence of good design in millinery. Of course, a hat can be sculptural, and doesn't have to follow conventional ideas of what a hat should look like, but at its core is its relationship to the head and face, indeed the whole person, of the wearer.

contemporary milliners

Writing in London in the first decade of the 21st century, it is encouraging to see how vibrant and diverse the millinery scene is today. Stephen Jones and Philip Treacy continue to be at the forefront, providing inspiration and leadership to each new generation of hat-makers. But there are several other contemporary milliners, each with their own highly individual approach and aesthetic. Perhaps one thing we all have in common is a passion for modern millinery, for using elements of traditional model millinery, but bringing it right up to date and making it desirable to new generations of hat-wearers.

FROM LEFT, TOP ROW Red suede sculpted hood by Karen Henriksen, from RCA MA collection 2003. This collection of sculptural millinery explored the traditional and everyday headwear of the past and present, transforming the ordinary into extraordinary. PHOTO: ROYAL COLLEGE OF ART

Red velour felt cap, from the Windswept Collection® by Karen Henriksen. This is a handmade version of the best-selling DEEPcap shape. Windswept® is a range of contemporary, unisex caps and hats, each developed from advanced pattern-cutting techniques that evolved from my RCA MA collection.

Black sinamay coolie with black and fire crin 'feathers' by Noel Stewart. In addition to his own collections, Noel is also known for his collaborations with some of the most exciting new fashion designers to emerge in recent years. PHOTO: MORGAN O' DONOVAN

BOTTOM ROW Ivory felt cap with scattered Swarovski crystals by Misa Harada. Misa's decadent men's line was launched in 2005, and reflects a growing demand for seriously stylish and adventurous mens' headwear. PHOTO COURTESY OF MISA HARADA

'Wave' by Yasmin Rizvi: dark-green wool-felt hat with feather fringe and silk flowers enclosed in blocked net. Yasmin draws from her multicultural background, reflecting the colours, shapes, textures and sensations absorbed from growing up in cities as diverse as Rome, Amsterdam, Lahore and New York. PHOTO: CAROLINE MARKS

RIGHT Black draped silk satin organza hat by Stephen Jones. This hat is from the 'Vanda' collection: an homage to millinery masterpieces from the past. PHOTO: PETER ASHWORTH

Basic tools and equipment for a millinery workroom.

2 equipment & materials

WHAT YOU WILL NEED

- Access to water supply, or simply a bowl of water
- Plant spray filled with water
- Small dry iron for millinery materials
- Steam iron for fabric
- Paper-cutting scissors (these should also be used for buckram and sinamay; never use good fabric-cutting scissors for these materials, as they will blunt them)
- Fabric-cutting scissors
- Small, pointed scissors
- Blocking cord with slip knot
- Dressmaking pins (long and fine)
- Pins for blocking (shorter and thicker, often described as household pins)
- Drawing pins
- Thimble

- Pencil/tailor's chalk
- Pliers/wire cutters
- Tape measure
- Millinery needles (sometimes sold as straw needles)
- Steamer or kettle
- Brushes for felt (firm toothbrushes work well, and a collection can be built up for use with different colours)
- Pressing pad (can simply be a piece of cotton fabric)

A NOTE ON THIMBLES

Using a thimble is something that probably isn't taught very much anymore; however, this is an essential piece of equipment for a milliner. Nearly all hand-stitching is carried out using one, and blocking would be almost impossible without one. It can be worn either on the index finger or the second finger; some people prefer to use the head of the thimble, others prefer the side, perhaps more like a tailor would. It might be necessary to try out different ways before finding the method that suits best – the important thing is to use one!

blocks

Blocks are forms made from wood on which the hat material is shaped. Since the decline of the millinery industry there are now fewer block-making companies in existence. However, those that are still in business have kept up to date, and acquiring blocks is perhaps more accessible and less expensive than might be expected. Generally, it is possible to choose from an extensive range from stock; alternatively, the block-maker will make to order from customers' own designs.

While blocks are clearly an essential piece of equipment for a milliner, it is not necessary to spend a fortune as an initial outlay. Over time, a collection of blocks can be built up, but to begin with, just one basic dome crown block and a versatile or favourite brim block will go a long way. Dome crown blocks are quite often found in second-hand and antique shops; but it is also a relatively small investment to have a new one made to one's own head size and specification.

A perhaps surprisingly small number of blocks have been used to make the project hats. In fact, the basic dome block has been used for five different hats in this book, and there are countless other designs that could emerge from just this one block.

A small collection of blocks. The three white blocks are handmade, using layers of buckram that have been built up and then stiffened using undiluted water-based stiffener, and covered with piece-felt or tarlatan to give a smooth finish. The darker woodblocks are old and have been purchased second-hand. The block at the far left is a classic trilby shape; this was used to make the hat on page 137.

sinamay

Sinamay is a new material for hats, having been introduced during the mid 1990s. Although at first it took a little time for milliners and hat factories to become used to it and perfect its treatment, it rapidly became very popular and has for some time completely dominated the occasion-hat industry. This is perhaps not surprising: it is light yet stiff, can be sculpted easily by hand, and dyes well – properties perfect for making hats. It also works very well as a light but firm base for feathers or even some fabrics – a lighter, transparent and more colourful alternative to buckram. The way it is woven also gives it more scope for being cut out into large shapes without being limited by the size of a hood as other straws are.

Sinamay is a type of straw, coming from the abaca (banana) plant, but unlike other straws it is woven like cloth and sold by the metre or by the roll rather than as basic unfinished hat bodies, or 'hoods'. Over the last decade, innovations have been added to the sinamay story – it is now available mixed with lurex, with silk, with a screen print applied, as two-tone sinamay, alternative weaves and also as a tangled web of sinamay threads.

Printed sinamay sculpted cap with stingray edge, from Elemental couture collection.

Rolls of sinamay.

straw

After sinamay, parasisal straw is probably the most popular straw for occasion wear. It is grown from the sisal plant, mostly in the Philippines, and then imported into China to be hand-woven. This is an industry that has existed for well over 100 years.

Parasisal is available to buy as hoods. There are two shapes to choose from – capeline and cone. A capeline has quite a small crown (top) section with a wide brim part, and is used for brimmed hats. A cone is more bell-shaped and is used for brimless or very small-brimmed hats and for crowns. Sometimes a cone and capeline might both be used for a hat. The classic hat on page 105 is made from a parasisal capeline.

Panama is also hand-woven (but in Ecuador) and is available at differing grades. Generally, these hoods are available only as capelines. Mostly found in plain colours, they are also available with contrasting colours, which shows off the weave perfectly. Paper panama is also quite widely available and is suitable for very casual, inexpensive hats.

A parasisal capeline and cone.

Panama straw hoods in two-tone and ivory, and a paper panama (at the back of the picture).

Stitched straws, or straw-plait hoods, are seen less now than woven, although this was the original type of straw going back many hundreds of years. Tuscany in Italy is famous as probably the original area for this straw-plaiting industry, and still supplies fine straw plait alongside some interesting synthetic versions. In England, Bedfordshire became the centre of the hat industry because of its own straw-plaiting industry, although the climate here produced a less fine straw than in Tuscany. Although this is now long gone, Luton, in Bedfordshire, remains the centre of the millinery industry in the UK. Here, there are still a few long-established millinery factories left, as well as suppliers and associated trades (block-maker and dyer, for example).

Stitched straw hoods – the black hood is an inexpensive version, while the natural is much finer, although not as fine as some stitched straws in the past would have been.

felt

Felt is a non-woven type of fabric composed of a compressed mass of fibres. These fibres originate from either the fleece of sheep (wool felt) or from rabbit and hare fur (fur felt). Like straw, it is also available to the milliner in the form of hoods – capelines and cones.

Wool felt is of course the less expensive option but doesn't have the luxurious feel of fur felt. Fur felt has a range of finishes to choose from: plain finish, with no pile but a very smooth look; velour (or peachbloom), with a velvety pile – this should be treated with care so as not to damage the pile; melusine, which is a longer hair with a silky look; and moufflon, which is longer-haired still but without the shine.

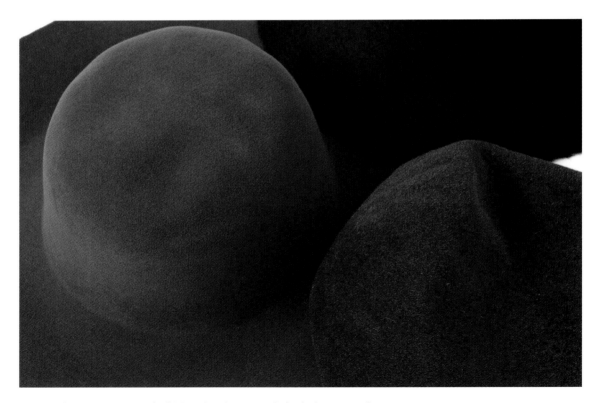

Textures of felt: the green plain fur felt here has almost a suede finish; the grey is velour; while just seen is a silky melusine in black.

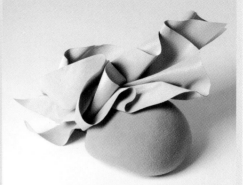

A sculpted hood in ivory moufflon felt with stitch detail inside, from Empire Lines couture collection.

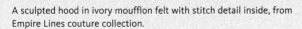

TOP Grey velour felt mini-beret, with a cascade of performance-nylon fabric. The crisp nylon adds a modern note to a classic 1950s-style shape. From Best in Show couture collection.
PHOTO: KEVIN DUTTON

ABOVE This mini-topper by Stephen Jones is made from a felt hood that has a candy-coloured print applied. Clever use has been made of the excess felt after blocking, to create a disciplined, co-ordinated trimming. PHOTO: PETER ASHWORTH

trimmings

SINAMAY

These sinamay trimmings have all been made using bias strips of various widths, with the exception of the white shredded sinamay in the centre, which is a strip cut on the straight grain and frayed extensively before being rolled up and stitched at the base.

FEATHERS

Feathers have been extremely fashionable for some time, either to trim a hat, or very often on their own, perching on the head. Coque feathers, from a cockerel, are very widely available in many colours, usually already stripped as seen here. The lilac ostrich feather is a spadone, which is much thinner and much less expensive than a prime. Hackle feathers, from a chicken, are usually available on a strip but are seen here mounted in a spray with coque. These mixed feather mounts, or sprays, are also widely available and provide a quick and easy but very effective trim.

A variety of feathers, clockwise from far left: deep-pink spray of hackle and stripped coque; two arrowhead quills shaped from basic turkey feathers; a bright-pink ostrich feather completely stripped to leave a plain spine; shiny black peacock brush; ivory marabou on a strip; an unstripped lilac ostrich feather; part of an ostrich boa; blue stripped coque; light-brown spiky goose feathers, known as biots.

Here, goose biots in three colours have been curled and randomly mixed to contrast with a fine black veiling, forming a toning trim for a simple square-shaped cloche hat.

PETERSHAM RIBBON

These are ridged ribbons made of cotton/viscose and are used for head fittings inside hats. This must be the cotton type of petersham rather than the more widely available version in polyester, which is not recommended for millinery work, as it needs to be capable of stretching, shrinking and curving to fit heads and hats. It can also be used as a trimming on the outside of a hat. There are various widths available, with the most common being 2.5 cm (1 in.), also known as no.5 size. The narrowest size generally available is 1.5 cm ($^5/_8$ in.), also known as no.3.

Vintage petersham, including striped versions (likely to be 100% cotton, rather than the modern cotton/viscose, and also occasionally silk) can sometimes be found at vintage outlets.

Rolls of petersham ribbon.

foundation materials

Buckram (seen as a rolled fabric at the back of the photograph below)
This is a very stiff cotton canvas that becomes very soft and pliable when wet. It is used as a foundation for blocked fabric hats and can also be cut out from flat and used for components in hats. One version of buckram is double-sided and fusible on both sides. The blue-and-white checked fabric in the centre of the picture has double-sided buckram sandwiched between. This is seen used as a peak for the cotton shirting cap on page 121.

Fusible cotton (staflex) and **domette** (seen folded in the centre of the picture)
These are used to help make fabrics firmer (particularly for cut and sewn hats) and also to provide padding between buckram and an outer fabric in blocked hats. Domette is thicker and softer than staflex.

Tarlatan
A very light but stiff cotton fabric. This is seen cut into narrow bias strips, which are used to cover a wire edge. It can also be used as a sew-in interlining for cut and sewn hats where a fusible option wouldn't be suitable.

Wire
Millinery wire is steel wire covered in either black or white cotton, available in half-kilo reels. The stiffness can vary – clearly the stiffer the wire, the better it will be at holding a shape. But sometimes only a softer wire is available; this at least has the advantage of being much easier to work with, although extra care must be taken to avoid kinks occurring during working and also when handling the finished hat.

Various fabrics and components that go into making a hat, before any trimmings or outer fabric.

3 basic techniques

Hats can be broadly split into two types: blocked, and cut-and-sewn, with quite significant differences in technique. Blocked hats are mostly based on traditional model millinery methods, whereas cut-and-sewn are based on garment-making methods. Most of the techniques in this chapter refer to blocked hats, but there are also some references to cut-and-sewn hats.

Use of abbreviations, throughout the book:
CF = centre front
CB = centre back

SEWING THREADS

Try to use the best-quality sewing thread you can. For most tasks, good-quality polyester thread is fine. But for certain techniques where there is to be a lot of ironing, only cotton thread should be used. A good example would be the buckram base for the silk headpiece, page 81; the hot iron required for really smoothing the tarlatan edge would melt any stitches made in polyester thread.

Note: Most of the instructional photographs for the basic techniques and later the project hats show contrasting-colour thread used; this is purely for clarity of course, and it should be assumed that matching thread would be used in reality!

bias

The bias is the diagonal part of a woven fabric, and is very flexible and stretchy, unlike the straight grain. The importance of the bias in millinery cannot be overstated. Cutting fabrics on the bias is one of the fundamental rules of millinery, and unlike perhaps some other rules it is rare that this one can ever be broken successfully.

Just as a bias-cut dress will fall and drape beautifully, a bias-cut piece of fabric will fit perfectly around the curved areas that are so prevalent in hats.

Reference is made throughout this book to bias strips; don't be tempted to try to use strips cut on the straight grain of the fabric in any of these cases, as this simply won't work!

To find the true bias in a woven fabric, make a diagonal fold, so that the straight grain running down the length (the warp) lines up to run parallel with the straight grain running across (the weft). The diagonal is the true bias.

Cutting a bias strip in sinamay.

head fitting for hats

TAKING A HEAD MEASUREMENT

Make sure that the tape measure sits around the head just above the ears. An average head size for women is around 57 cm (22 in.). As long as the tape measure isn't pulled too tightly (it should feel comfortable and exactly how you would want to wear the hat), for most blocked hats this should be the exact measurement to work with. For cut and sewn hats, particularly in thicker fabrics and/or if the hat is to be worn pulled down deeply over the ears, for example, then ease should be added. This could be from 0.5 cm ($^3/_{16}$ in.) to as much as 1.5 cm ($^5/_8$ in.).

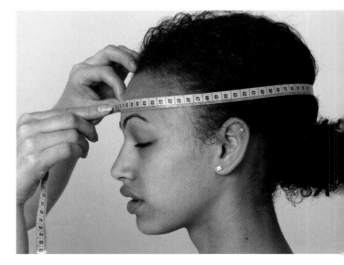

Taking a head measurement.

ATTACHING A PETERSHAM HEAD FITTING

1. Cut a piece of petersham ribbon the length of the head size, adding 3 cm (1¼ in.) for overlapping (1.5 cm/⅝ in. at each end).

2. To achieve a smooth finish, the petersham can be curved slightly by ironing.

3. Pin together and try the petersham on before pinning in place into the head fitting of the hat. The pinned ends can remain as a simple folded join at the CB, with the raw ends behind. Make sure that the lower edge of the petersham isn't protruding lower than the head-fitting edge, as this would make it visible when the hat is worn.

4. Stitch in place using a very tiny stab-stitch on the lower edge of the petersham, and no more than 0.75 cm (⁵⁄₁₆ in.) apart on the wrong side.

Note: It is best to fit the petersham to the correct head size before attaching to the hat, as the head-fitting part of the hat isn't necessarily the exact size required. There may be a difference between the two of up to about a centimetre either way before there is any real problem in fitting them together. This is true for cut-and-sewn as well as blocked hats.

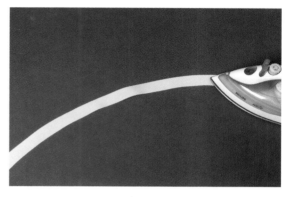

Curving a Petersham ribbon.

A Petersham head-fitting stitched to a straw brim.

securing a headpiece

ELASTIC

Hat elastic is very thin and tubular in shape. The required length (this can vary but is likely to be around 30 cm/12 in.) should be cut from the roll and knotted at each end, then stitched with one end at each side of the hat. The stitches need to be strong and secure but very discreet. In some cases it is necessary to come through to the right side of the hat when stitching in place – here extra care should be taken to keep the stitches as tiny and even as possible.

It is also possible to purchase ready-made lengths of elastic with metal ends fitted – these are designed simply to slot through the stitching on the petersham ribbon.

When wearing a hat or headpiece with elastic fitted, first position the hat in place on the head with the elastic to the back. Then push the elastic down to the nape of the neck, pulling the hair over. The hair can also be rearranged at the sides to cover the elastic. Even if it is visible, black elastic blends well on most medium to dark hair colours; white elastic can be dyed to blend in with lighter hair.

WIRE HEADBAND
A wire headband can be handmade (see bridal headdress, page 111) or a purchased Alice band could be used (as in the crin veil, page 72). In either case, the standard length for a wire headband is about 34 cm (13$^1/_2$ in.). This is the measurement from just behind the top part of the ear, going over the head and down to the corresponding place on the other side. It is not likely to vary by very much, although it is worth checking on particularly small or large heads!

COMB
Alternatively, for small fascinators, a comb can work well (see sinamay headpiece, page 100). The method that is used will probably depend on the headpiece in question but might also depend on hairstyle and thickness of hair.

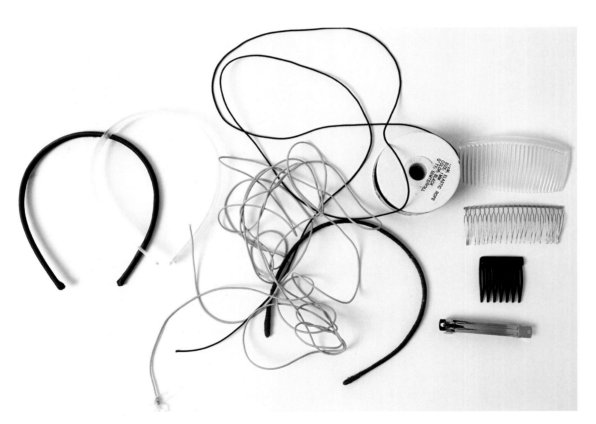

Hairbands, elastic and combs are all alternatives for securing small hats and headpieces to the head.

use of stiffeners

The traditional felt and straw stiffeners require very strict guidelines for use – always make sure that the room is well-ventilated. Another important point is that when wet, thinners should never come into contact with water.

In contrast, water-based stiffener is a white, PVA glue-type stiffener, which is used diluted with water. It is completely harmless and the same rules regarding ventilation do not apply here.

Either felt stiffener or water-based stiffener will work on felt. In either case, it is applied only to the wrong side of the felt, and generally to the crown part only, before blocking. Apply sparingly and allow to dry, repeating with another layer if a firm finish is required. In this way, there is less likely to be a visible residue, although water-based stiffener does tend to leave the felt with quite a rough finish. If this is the case, a lining can be inserted into the finished hat if required. If the brim also needs to be stiffened, felt stiffener is really the better option as this will seep in without altering the surface, as long as it is applied sparingly. However, in the case of double-sided velour or melusine felts where there is no wrong side, stiffener should not be applied. Generally, these tend to be quite thick and firm and don't need to be stiffened anyway.

Straw stiffener, or varnish, is the preferred stiffener for straw, giving it a clear shine and flexibility. It should be painted onto the right side of the straw while still on the block, but only once the straw has completely dried following the blocking process. Once off the block, the wrong side can also be varnished if required.

Water-based stiffener is ideal for sinamay. It should be painted onto the sinamay while on the block, straight after blocking (no need to wait for it to dry), and should be ironed when the stiffener has almost dried. If it has dried completely, just dab or spray a little water first before ironing. Preferably, use a clean dry iron applied directly to the sinamay; with light colours, check an inconspicuous area first in case the iron leaves scorch marks, and if so use a pressing cloth. When painted on, the surface becomes white, but this usually disappears as it dries. Sometimes if the stiffener was quite concentrated, some whiteness might remain even when dry, but this too will disappear when it is ironed.

If straw varnish is not available, water-based stiffener can also be used on straw, but care should be taken as it can leave the straw rather brittle and prone to tearing. Treat in the same way as for sinamay. It will also give the straw a more matt finish than straw stiffener, even after ironing.

blocking techniques

PREPARING BLOCKS BEFORE USE

It is important to cover the block with a fine plastic bag or cling film before starting to work on it. This will help protect both the block and the material from possible dye residue, and will prevent materials from sticking to the block.

BLOCKING FELT HOODS

Before blocking felt, it is a good idea to moisten the inside of the hood first – simply spray thoroughly with water on the inside of the hood, then roll it up and place inside an airtight plastic bag. This can be left for several hours, even overnight is fine (leave in the fridge in this case, to preserve it). The stiffer the felt, the longer it should be left.

Steam is used to soften felt for blocking. This can either come from a steamer or a kettle; alternatively, steam can be generated by using a wet cloth and hot iron. The wool-felt hat on page 61 is blocked using the latter method. Generally, this works well for felts with little or no pile, such as wool felt or plain fur felt, and also those with a long pile such as melusine. It is not recommended for velour (peachbloom) felts, however, as the pile can be permanently damaged. For the same reason, be careful when spraying water on the inside of velours; take care not to get water on the right side. It isn't necessary to be so careful with the other felts – these can even be immersed in water without causing damage. Velour-felt hoods should be steamed using a kettle or steamer; when holding the felt in the steam, keep your hands low and out of the way of the heat as much

as possible. First let the hood sit over the steam on its own before placing it onto the block. Then pull it into place and pin. Then keep returning the felt to the steam (leaving it attached to the block now) to re-soften each area to be blocked. The steam can also help remove any marks left by a blocking cord: hold a brush in the steam for a few seconds and then use it to brush over the cord line.

BLOCKING STRAW HOODS

Straw can also be softened using steam, although simply immersing the straw hood in water is probably the easier and more efficient method. It is then placed straight onto the block, without the need to be left in a bag to absorb moisture. (See the classic straw hat, page 105, for blocking a straw crown and brim.) When pulling the straw at a particular point on the outside edge, the circular bias weave will become apparent as the diagonal strands straighten out.

BLOCKING SINAMAY

Sinamay should be used in either two or three layers. A brim is generally blocked from squares of sinamay, although depending on the shape, bias strips can also be used, with a neat seam at CB. Crowns can be blocked in one piece, also from squares, although this is recommended only for very shallow crowns as it is impossible to get a smooth finish around a sideband in this way. For most crowns, it is better to block in two pieces: squares for the tip and bias strips for the sideband. (See the sinamay pillbox, page 93, for more details on blocking a crown in two pieces.)

USING PINS AND BLOCKING CORDS

Whatever the material to be blocked, the pins must enter the block at a wide angle from the material, otherwise they will not be effective in holding it securely in place. It can take a little while to get used to blocking with straight pins, but it is worth persevering! Drawing pins should only be used on the base or inside edge of a block, or around a collar on a brim for a head fitting, as they make larger holes in the block and can also leave rust marks. They are also less effective in most cases.

Pins holding a straw crown in place. Angled like this, they will stop the straw from shrinking back to leave wrinkles.

Pins holding a felt brim in place. These also enter the block at a wide angle from the felt.

Using a blocking cord: this is simply a length of cord, preferably nylon, with a loop secured at one end. The other end is threaded through and pulled tightly, then secured with a pin into the block. This is especially useful for head fittings.

closing a wire

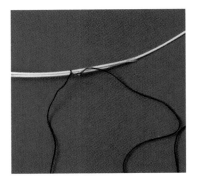 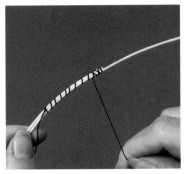 

Wire is used throughout the project hats. In some cases, it can be simply stitched in place, with extra care being taken at the join of wire (which is usually placed at the CB) to make sure that the ends are well-secured. But in many cases where a very neat finish is required, it is better to close the wire separately from the hat.

1. Cut the required length of wire with pliers, adding about 7 cm (2³/₄ in.) for the overlap. To remove the spring, smooth out the wire by running it firmly between your fingers but taking care not to allow any kinks.

2. Make a temporary join first, with Sellotape – use two or three pieces to hold in place. Then tie a long piece of thread with a double knot around the centre of the join.

3. Remove the Sellotape from one side of the join, and wrap one of the long ends of thread very tightly around the wire. Double-back when reaching the end of the join and return to the centre. Secure with another double knot.

4. Repeat for the other side of the join, and cut away the excess ends of thread.

millinery stitches

STITCHING WIRE

There are two variations for stitching wire onto an edge, before adding a bind.

Note: In either case, wire attached to felt can sit along the very edge, as the thickness of the felt provides an ideal platform for it.

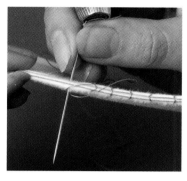

The main wire stitch is similar to blanket stitch: for each stitch, as the needle goes through the material, it should also go through the looped thread so that when pulled through, the thread forms a knot over the wire. The stitches should be up to 1 cm (⅜ in.) apart.

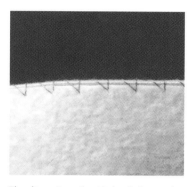

The alternative wire stitch: stitch over the wire, then go forward to form another overstitch. To make it secure, another stitch is made here before going forward again. Repeat this each time, creating v-shapes along the edge.

In contrast, wire attached to straw (and also buckram) should sit just on the inside edge. Note also that blanket stitch is preferred for straw, rather than the alternative wire stitch, which can sometimes tear the straw.

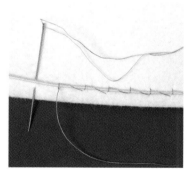

If a turned edge rather than a bind is required for a felt brim, the wire should be stitched about 0.75 cm (⁵⁄₁₆ in.) from the edge, on the inside or downside of the brim. This stitch is similar to the one shown above right, but take the needle only through the thickness of the felt each time, not right through to the other side.

The edge of the felt is then turned over the wire, pressed, and slip-stitched in place, with the edge of the felt treated as though it were a folded fabric. However, if the felt is very thin, it might be better to use an invisible stab stitch to hold the turned edge in place.

For stitching a wire to a sinamay brim, machine-stitching over the wire using a zigzag stitch is an efficient way of working with a material that causes the thread to tangle badly when hand-stitching. It also gives a crisp, clean finish. Even when the rest of the hat is hand-stitched, I would still always prefer this way of wiring a sinamay brim. It is worth considering that what is essentially a modern fabric doesn't necessarily have to be treated as a more traditional fabric might. After stitching over the wire, the sinamay edge is turned over and pressed, then straight-stitched to hold it in place, before attaching the bind. In this case, it is a self-bind that has been prepared by ironing and then hand-stitched.

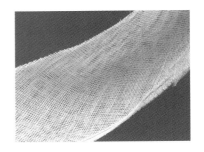

A cross section of a sinamay brim, showing wire machine-stitched, then with the edge turned, and finally with a hand-stitched self-bind.

SLIP STITCH

This is a very important invisible stitch in millinery and is used extensively for joining a folded fabric to another surface, or joining two folded edges together. It is worth spending time perfecting this stitch to create a beautiful and professional finish.

Example – to finish a fabric bind at the edge of a brim

The classic straw hat on page 105 has a rolled edge, but an alternative would be a bind in the same silk as the trim. Here, the first edge of fabric has been machine-stitched along the top side of the brim edge. The other fabric edge is now to be slip-stitched in place on the underside of the brim to close the bind. (See also straw visor, page 51, for more information on fabric binds.)

1. The needle and thread is taken along the folded edge of silk for no more than 0.75 cm ($^5/_{16}$ in.).

2. It is then taken directly opposite, into the straw, without allowing the needle to move forward. Here, go through just a strand or two of straw, and/or through the machine-stitching.

3. Repeat this for each stitch, remembering that the needle should go directly from the fabric to the straw and vice versa. It is this that ensures the thread is invisible. It is also important to pull the seam closed as you stitch but without pulling too tightly as this will cause the fabric to pucker. And the needle should only point forwards; don't allow it to pull back on itself, as this can cause the fabric to tear. From time to time, if necessary to make it extra secure, or if it is difficult to get hold of the straw properly, the needle can be brought right through to the right side of the brim. Make sure that the stitch here is very tiny and sits right at the edge of the machined seam.

Slip stitch is often also used for attaching a lining (see silk headpiece, page 81, and Cossack hat, page 77), and for

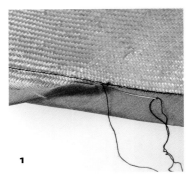

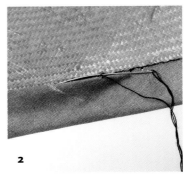

joining two folded pieces of fabric together (this is seen in the rouleau for the crin mask, page 72).

STAB STITCH

This is also an important millinery stitch and is invisible, or almost invisible: a very tiny stitch on the right side. Angle the needle forward slightly each time to ensure that it doesn't just go back through the same hole. The stitches can be up to 1 cm ($^3/_8$ in.) apart on the wrong side. It is used for stitching petersham head fittings and also, for example, for invisibly joining a sinamay sideband and tip (see sinamay pillbox, page 93).

Another version is where both sides must be invisible, for example, a bind – again angle the needle forward as it enters the fabric each time, on both sides. The needle angled forward like this also helps speed up the process.

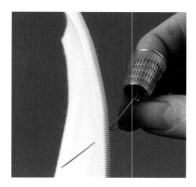

While this stitch is quite easy with sinamay, as the texture helps conceal the thread quite easily, it is more advanced and extremely time-consuming when used for a petersham bind. But this does give a beautiful, couture look when compared with a machine-stitched bind.

BACKSTITCH

This is a very secure, strong stitch, often used for joining a crown and brim, or for joining a buckram extension to a crown (but see note below). The stitch at the front can be quite long, up to about 1.5 cm ($^5/_8$ in.). At the back, the stitch should go backwards up to about 0.75 cm ($^5/_{16}$ in.) and so will come out about halfway through the stitch at the front. Repeat this each time until there is an unbroken line of thread at the front and a running stitch effect at the back. An alternative to backstitch is a vertical stitch I prefer to use when adding an extension to a crown, where the stitch goes just over the edge of the buckram – into the straw, in this case. The stitches will be diagonal at the back.

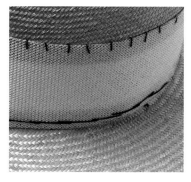

OVERSTITCH

Pieces of felt can be joined together edge to edge, rather than with a seam allowance. This technique might be used if there is insufficient felt, or the shape requires the hood to be used with a seam, or sometimes a small felt hat can be made from flat patterns if they fit onto a hood.

With right sides together, make tiny stitches over each edge of felt, and very close together.

When turned to the right side, the stitches are hardly seen, and can be further concealed by rubbing the point of a needle over the seam to lift the pile of the felt.

FINISHING OFF (French knot)

To finish off a line of stitching, bring the needle through to the wrong side and make a very small stitch (not going right through the fabric). Before the thread has been pulled through completely, take the needle through the remaining loop of thread, then continue to pull it through quite tightly. Repeat this twice, before trimming away the thread.

MACHINE STITCHES

For cut-and-sewn hats, the pieces of fabric are stitched together by machine. Use plenty of pins to hold the two fabric pieces in place. A tacking (basting) stitch can be made first, although I prefer only to use pins. The pins should sit at a right angle to the seam being stitched – it would be very difficult to control the fabric and stitch accurately if the pins were running lengthways.

Pinning a tip and sideband together: note that there are tabs, or tiny cuts, along the top edge of the sideband. These allow it to fit perfectly along the curved edge of the tip.

With most fabrics, it is possible to stitch over the pins, but if the fabric marks easily, simply remove each pin just before the foot reaches it. If stitching over the pins, the stitch length should be medium to long rather than short, to avoid hitting them, although this can still happen very occasionally.

After stitching, it is usually more effective to use topstitching as a way of finishing, rather than ironing seams. Depending on the type of seam and the effect required, topstitching can be applied down each side of the seam with the seam allowance opened, or on one side of the seam with the allowance pushed over to that side only. The small amount of excess fabric should be trimmed away afterwards to avoid unnecessary bulk.

Alternatively, the seams can be ironed, although this can be quite awkward on some shapes, especially at later stages in the making. Use a pressing pad underneath, or sometimes the hat can be placed over a block and moved around as necessary. It is nearly always advisable to use a pressing cloth between fabric and iron to avoid the fabric becoming shiny.

linings

The white lining at the top of the picture here is a standard purchased lining made from a bias strip simply pleated to fit a smallish round tip. Because of the flexibility of the bias, it will fit most hats, although would probably require some pleats at the head fitting inside very small-fitting hats.

Underneath are two linings that have been handmade. Again, a bias strip has been used, but this is gathered in quite tightly by hand and then a very tiny tip is attached to the reverse. This type of lining requires a slightly deeper bias strip as it has to reach almost to the centre of the tip when inside the crown. It makes a beautiful finish inside a model hat, and of course can be made to an exact head size.

On the right is a half-lining designed to cover just a sideband rather than a whole crown. The bias strip in this case simply has small box pleats at CF and CB to allow a perfect fit. This lining has been used for the classic straw hat on page 105.

Each of the cut-and-sewn hats have lining made from the same pattern pieces as the outer crown. Strictly speaking, separate, slightly smaller pattern pieces should be cut for the linings, but this isn't absolutely necessary – instead simply take a slightly larger seam allowance when stitching the lining pieces together.

introduction to the project hats

Most of the project hats here could be considered timeless – these classic styles form a great foundation on which to build and experiment. The Basic techniques chapter will also provide more detail or alternative methods. For the cut-and-sewn hats, refer to the pattern-cutting chapter at the end of the book for the relevant patterns.

Millinery is a relatively inexpensive subject to embark on initially – a lot can be achieved with only the most basic equipment. Just three blocks were used for six of these hats, with the basic dome block used for five different hats!

Materials and equipment particular to each hat are listed for each project; these are in addition to the basic equipment required such as needles and pins, scissors, etc. (see equipment & materials, page 19).

4 protection

corduroy cap

- 0.3 m (12 in.) corduroy (150 cm/59 in. wide)
- 0.3 m (12 in.) quilted lining
- Matching threads
- 30 x 30 cm (12 x 12 in.) fusible interlining
- Petersham head fitting
- 6-section crown and peak pattern pieces (see page 131)
- Sewing machine with heavy-duty needle fitted

This cap has lots of volume and can be pulled down deep for extra warmth. This is a particularly inexpensive hat to make, as it uses such a small amount of fabric. The tweed cap alternative seen on page 59 has eight sections, which allows for a smoother more rounded shape.

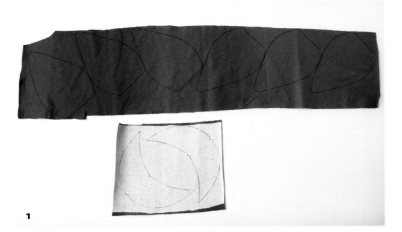

1

1. The corduroy used here is very heavy and doesn't require any interlining for the main part of the cap. Even with this fabric, though, the peak needs some stiffening. In this case, fusible cotton (Staflex) has been used on each of the two peak pieces. Place the square of Staflex on the wrong side of the corduroy at one end, and cut away the corduroy here from the rest of the fabric. Use a hot iron to press the Staflex, working outwards from the centre. To ensure adhesion, avoid moving the fabric until it has cooled completely.

Meanwhile, the six section pieces can be cut out of the remaining fabric; these should be cut on the cross. With corduroy, as with stripes, it is best to lay three with the grain lines running down the length of the fabric (i.e. with the corduroy ridges), and three with the grain lines running across. This will give a chevron effect when the pieces are sewn together alternately. Make sure that the two sets of fabric section pieces are kept separate.

2. Take one fabric section from each set and sew together, right sides together, along one long edge. Repeat with another pair. The final two pieces should remain separate for now.

3. Open each seam and topstitch down each side, then trim away the excess. This will keep the

3

seams smooth and flat, and suits the casual fabric very well. The small amount of excess fabric should be trimmed away afterwards to avoid unnecessary bulk. Now take the last two sections and add one to each of the pairs. Make sure that the correct one is attached each time, so that the chevron effect continues.

4

5

4. Open the seams, topstitch and trim as before. There are now two halves of the cap to be joined. Pin them together, starting at the centre. In order to get as perfect a match as possible here, take one of the halves and push a pin through the exact spot where the two seams cross each other, from the wrong side. Then continue pushing this pin through the corresponding point on the other half, this time with the right side upwards, so that the right sides of each half are now pressed against each other.

5. The two pieces can now be pinned as normal, and the holding pin removed ready for stitching. A line can be marked here, if necessary, to aid the stitching.

6. After stitching this final long seam, open it out and topstitch again down each side. Turn the cap through to the right side.

6

7. Now return to the fabric/Staflex for the peak. Two pieces are cut, on the bias, and stitched together.

8. This seam is also opened and topstitched on each side to give a really smooth edge. Afterwards, trim away the excess and iron flat.

9. The lining for this cap is quilted, for extra warmth. Cut out the six sections and stitch them together, following the same process as for the corduroy.

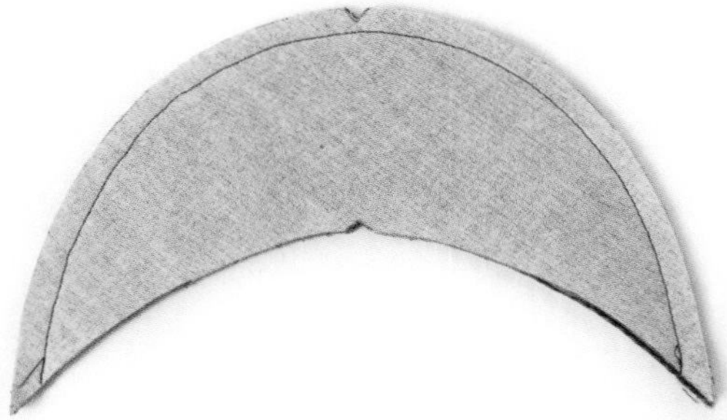

7

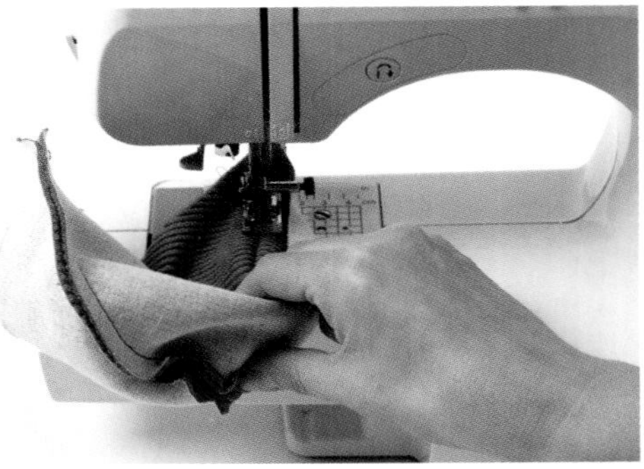

8

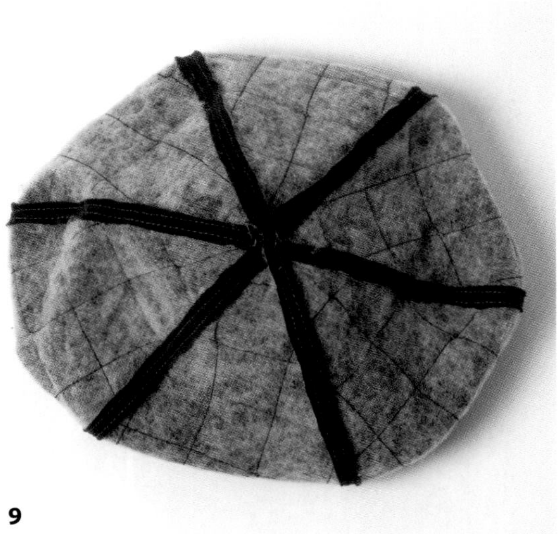

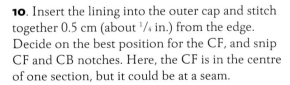

9

10. Insert the lining into the outer cap and stitch together 0.5 cm (about $^{1}/_{4}$ in.) from the edge. Decide on the best position for the CF, and snip CF and CB notches. Here, the CF is in the centre of one section, but it could be at a seam.

Note: For a more couture finish, the lining can be left separate for now and slip-stitched in place behind the petersham head fitting, when everything else is complete.

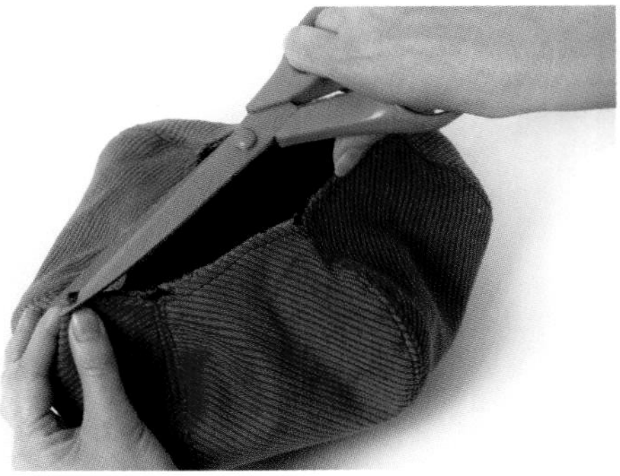

10

11. Next, pin the peak in place, matching the CF notches, and stitch these together.

12. Finally, the petersham head fitting is added, 1 cm ($^3/_8$ in.) in from the edge. Stitch very close to the lower edge of the petersham, removing each pin as the machine foot reaches them. Afterwards, the small amount of fabric excess can be trimmed away next to the first line of stitching behind the petersham.

13. The finished corduroy cap is seen here, alongside an 8-section version in wool tweed (also seen on page 59), and a baseball-type cap made in a luxurious wool/cashmere.

11

12

13

panama straw visor

WHAT YOU WILL NEED

- ▶ 1 panama straw hood
- ▶ Millinery wire
- ▶ Bias strip of tarlatan
- ▶ Bias strip of cotton fabric for binds, approx. 5 cm (2 in.) by 80 cm (3½ in.) (this is for a 1 cm (⅜ in.) bind – the width of the bias strip should be at least five times whatever the finished width of bind is required to be)
- ▶ Matching threads
- ▶ Hat elastic
- ▶ Visor pattern piece (see page 136)
- ▶ Sewing machine – recommended but not essential

A stylish but comfortable visor that provides protection from the sun. It is worn sloping down from the top of the head rather than with a head fitting, which allows the forehead to breathe. The hand-finished bind adds a couture note to an otherwise casual, practical hat.

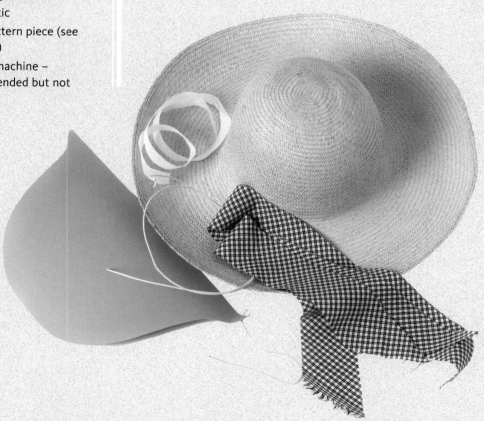

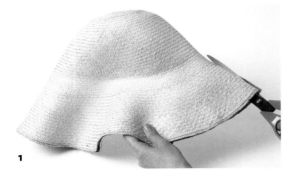

1. Start by cutting the straw hood in half.

2. One half must now be flattened out completely (cut away the top part first, where the weave is particularly tight). Use a damp cloth and hot iron, then use the iron alone to help dry the straw.

3. When placing the pattern piece on the straw, try to position it centrally, so that the weave is symmetrical.

Once the visor shape has been cut out, it might be necessary to iron it again, especially at the sides, which sit on what was the waisted part of the hood. When completely dry, straw varnish can be applied to each side.

4. Although the varnish will help, the straw will still be prone to fraying. So a strip of tarlatan immediately stitched to the edge will prevent this and will also provide a neat, straight edge on which to attach the wire. This is of course contrary to the more usual practice of wiring and then covering the wire with tarlatan.

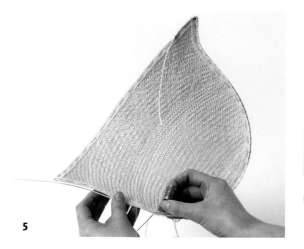

5

6

7

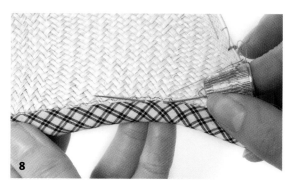

8

5. The wire should be shaped and bent to fit the visor on the inside edge, and stitched in place. Afterwards, shape the visor by gently bending the wire to form a natural curve. Check the shape in the mirror: it should fit comfortably with the points just behind the ears. For smaller head sizes the shape can be closed slightly.

6. Take the bias strip of fabric and pin it onto the top side of the visor, along the long curved edge, with the right side facing down. Pull the fabric fairly taut, and make sure that about 0.5 cm (about ¼ in.) of fabric turns over the edge onto the underside; this provides a tension which helps the fabric to stay in place while stitching, and will also provide an extra layer to cushion the wire. Extra pins can be placed along the more intricate curved areas close to each point, to avoid the fabric pleating as it is stitched.

7. It is preferable to machine-stitch this seam, as this gives a smooth, clean finish. Use the foot as a guide, or draw in a stitching line in pencil 0.7 cm (⁵/₁₆ in.) from the wire (this will give a 1 cm (³/₈ in.) width on the right side). If hand-stitching is preferred, make sure it is a small backstitch as straight as possible, almost mimicking a machine stitch. To close the bind, pull the fabric over the edge and fold in so that the folded edge runs directly along the machine stitches on the underside. Cut away the remaining part of the bias strip – this will be used for the bind at the back edge of the visor. The fabric ends can simply be trimmed to lie flush with the points of the visor; they will be covered by this second bind.

8. This folded edge is now slip-stitched in place. See page 38 for more details on slip stitch.

9. The other bias strip can now be machined in place along the back section of the visor, in the same way, making sure that there is excess fabric at each end. This time the excess is folded in and secured to the tarlatan with small hand stitches. At these points, the hat elastic is also stitched in place. Finally, this bind is completed by folding in and slip-stitching as before.

9

10. The other side of the straw hood can be used to make a second visor. The alternative style shown here has been cut the other way on the straw, using the waisted part of the hood to shape the visor upwards. The bind here is a printed sinamay, hand-stitched, and slightly wider at the back edge.

10

A NOTE ON FABRIC BINDS

For this visor, the bind is best completed in two pieces because of the shape, whereas a fabric bind on a brim would of course be made in one piece. For this, the bias strip is first pulled around the brim edge to find the required length (hold in place with a pin) – this is more reliable than simply measuring, as fabrics will differ in the amount of stretch they have. Then a CB seam is machine-stitched and pressed open. The bind is placed back onto the brim edge, with the right side facing down onto the top side of the brim, as indicated for the visor, and stitched in the same way. (See also millinery stitches, page 38, for more information on slip-stitching.)

cotton rain hat

WHAT YOU WILL NEED

- 1 m (39 in.) coated cotton
- 0.5 m (19½ in.) satin lining
- Matching threads
- Petersham head fitting
- Wide-brim pattern piece, tapered sideband and matching tip pattern pieces (see page 122)
- Sewing machine

The cotton used for this hat has a showerproof coating to provide protection from the rain; for a more high-tech version, performance nylon fabric would be a very light option. This shape would also make a great sun hat in linen or a printed cotton.

Tools and equipment.

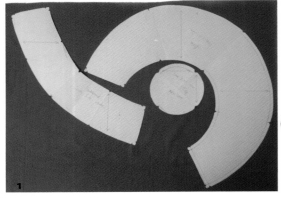

1. The pattern pieces should be laid so that the grain lines are parallel with the straight grains of the fabric. Once these three pieces have been outlined, the brim piece must be moved and replaced further down the fabric to cut a second piece. The sideband and tip pattern pieces should be used again for the lining fabric.

2. Stitch the CB seams on the two brim pieces and the sideband. The lining sideband can also be stitched now. Afterwards, open each CB seam and topstitch down each side.

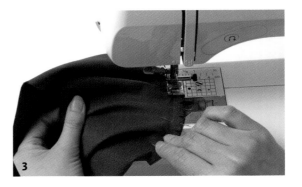

3. Cut tabs along the top edge of the sideband and pin this to the tip, matching notches first, and filling in between (see page 40). If the fabric does not mark easily, the pins can remain in place and be stitched over. But in this case, each pin should be removed just before the machine foot reaches it.

4

5

6

7

8

4. Rather than opening this seam, as before, here both layers of the seam allowance have been pushed onto the sideband and topstitched close to the seam. Trim away the excess here. Repeat this process for the lining, taking a slightly larger seam allowance.

5. Turn the crown through to the right side and insert the lining. These are stitched together 0.5 cm (about $^1/_4$ in.) from the edge. Alternatively, the lining can remain separate for now, and be slip-stitched in place behind the petersham when the hat is complete.

6. The brim pieces are placed right sides together and stitched around the outside edge – pin first, matching all notches and CB seams.

7. This seam is now opened and topstitched on each side.

8. The brim has spiral topstitching throughout to add firmness. Trim away the excess seam allowance and re-close the brim, smoothing the layers together and pinning through both layers every so often. Work from the outside inwards, finally matching notches and CB seam around the head-fitting edge. This will prevent the fabric from moving while topstitching the spiral. To begin, start at the CB, stitching very close to the edge, moving in gradually to about 0.5 cm (about $^1/_4$ in.) from the edge (use the foot as a guide). When the CB is reached again, just continue

9

around without stopping. Continue stitching in this way, using the edge of the foot as a guide against the previous row. Because the brim is shorter at the back, it will be necessary to have extra rows around the sides and front as you approach the head-fitting edge.

9. Snip into the head-fitting edge of the brim before pinning and stitching the crown and brim together. The stitch line for this seam should be slightly closer to the edge than the usual 1 cm (³/₈ in.) seam allowance – about 0.7 cm (⁵/₁₆ in.) is ideal.

10. Finally, stitch the petersham in place, this time with the usual 1cm (³/₈ in.) seam allowance.

11. Trim away behind the petersham as far as the previous line of stitching.

12. The finished hat.

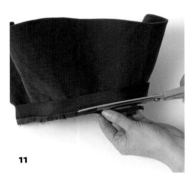

10

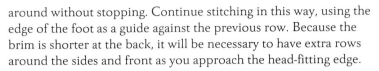

11

12

gallery – protection

ABOVE LEFT An eight-section cap, in wool tweed; the extra sections mean that a more rounded shape can be achieved than with six.

ABOVE A modern classic, this sun hat by Noel Stewart has a grey jersey crown with a black crin-fabric wide brim.
PHOTO: MORGAN O' DONOVAN

LEFT The cap here is made from a warm and hard-wearing military-type wool. The shallow sideband is tapered in slightly, like the cotton rain hat, to fit a small circular tip. The flap can be worn up or down and is backed with co-ordinating brushed cotton to provide both warmth and comfort.

5 attitude

wool-felt hat

WHAT YOU WILL NEED

▶ 1 wool felt capeline
▶ Petersham head fitting
▶ Approx. 4 m (13 ft) narrow
  satin ribbon
▶ Narrow strip cut from an A4
  acetate sheet for trim
▶ Dome crown block
▶ Large brim block
▶ Kettle or steamer
▶ Iron, bowl of water and
  pressing cloth

The iconic trilby and its close relative the fedora (which has a slightly wider brim) are constantly being reinvented and resurrected, both in womenswear and menswear.

This wide-brimmed hat has a suggestion of a trilby in its crown, but has been made the cheat's way, by using a dome crown block rather than an actual trilby block.

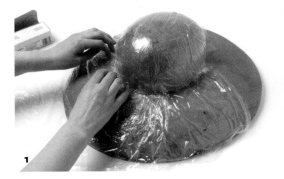

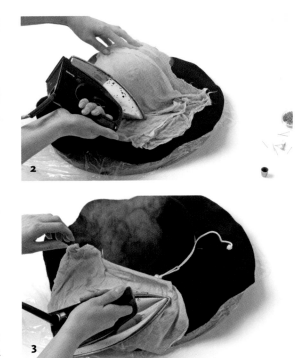

1. Stiffen the inside of the felt hood on the crown part only and leave to dry (see page 33). When completely dry, spray the inside of the felt with water, roll up the hood and place in an airtight plastic bag.

In the meantime, prepare the blocks: this hat has been blocked in one piece, rather than the crown and brim being blocked separately. The collar must be removed from the brim block, so that the crown block can be attached here instead: make sure the CF and CB marks on each block line up, then simply use strips of good-quality Sellotape to hold the crown block in place. The blocks now need to be covered in cling film, which is easier to handle on this large shape than plastic bags would be.

2. The felt hood for this hat has been blocked using a wet cloth and hot iron rather than a steamer or kettle to generate steam. This has the advantage of working on the blocks on the table top rather than having to lift them to hold in the steam. This method also tends to thicken and stiffen the felt, which is helpful as the brim doesn't have any stiffener applied.

Make sure that the cloth is thoroughly wet, place onto a top section of the crown, and then place the iron briefly on top of the cloth, making sure that it does not touch the felt directly. This can be repeated once or twice before the cloth dries. Take care when removing the cloth, as it will now be very hot: pick it up at the edge and replace it in

the bowl of water ready to reuse. Repeat the process all over the crown, pulling and smoothing the felt each time. The felt will be very soft and easily manipulated to the shape of this block; stretch just as much as required but no more. As you work on the lower part of the crown, place a blocking cord around and secure this by pinning through the end into the crown block.

3. The brim now should be treated in the same way; again, don't be tempted to stretch the felt more than is required to achieve a smooth surface. In this case, the finished brim is not very wide and doesn't require the full amount of felt, or the use of the whole of the brim block. By not stretching the felt more than required, it retains its thickness and stiffness. As the felt is blocked before the edge of the brim, pins rather than a blocking cord must be used to keep it in place. Make sure that the heads of the pins are pointing outwards, away from the crown.

4. The felt will take quite some time to dry – it is probably best to leave overnight. Before removing it from the blocks, CF, CB and the outline for the finished brim should be marked with tailor's chalk. The brim for this hat is slightly longer over the right eye, so that even when worn straight on the head, there is an 'attitude' to the hat, and when tilted slightly to the right, the effect is more extreme. From the CF mark, measure along to the left about 7 cm (2³/₄ in.) (so it is the right-hand side when worn). From here measure out 10.5 cm (4¹/₈ in.) – this will be the longest part of the brim.

5. Continue measuring out from the head fitting to complete the brim outline. From the initial mark the line should slope in very gradually, with the rest of the brim measuring 8 cm (3¹/₈ in.). At this time, also mark the CB on the drawn outline.

6. The brim can now be removed from the block and cut along the drawn line. This can

either be cut with scissors to give a sharp finish (try to cut in one action, rather than a series of cuts), or by using a sewing machine to perforate and give a more torn effect. Set the machine to a very short stitch length and fit a large-size needle without any thread. Starting at the CB, machine along the drawn line until you reach the CB again (go back and forward a couple of times here so that this part is extra-perforated). Then make a cut here, from the edge of the felt to the perforated line, and tear away the excess felt.

7. The crown is now shaped into a suggestion of a trilby-style hat. This is achieved first by softening the crown with steam, this time using a steamer or kettle. Hold the crown over the steam for about 30 seconds **(a)**, then remove and immediately make indentations with your fingers **(b)**. Don't stop holding the felt in this way until it is dry and has firmed up again. It might be necessary to work on each side separately. If you are not completely happy

8

9

10

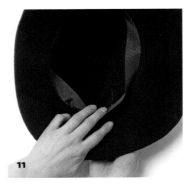

11

with the shape, or if the dents need to be deeper, the process can be repeated until it is right; try the hat on in the mirror to check the effect.

8. The petersham ribbon is inserted into the head fitting – pin in place first, with one end folded in over the other at the CB. This will be slightly more awkward to stitch than when working on a brim separate from a crown. Also, the stitch in this case needs to be as invisible as possible on both sides, as the ribbon trim may not completely cover the outside stitches.

9. Before arranging the ribbon trim, check that the original chalk mark is still visible to the right of the CF. A pin can be added here for extra clarity. This will be the focal point for the trim, where the satin ribbon starts and ends and where the acetate bow will be attached. The narrow satin ribbon is now wrapped around the crown, crossing over fairly randomly, and starting and finishing at the pin. Secure this in place with

tiny stab stitches, at the edge of the ribbon, and going right through the felt to the wrong side. While very tiny on the ribbon edge, the stitches can be up to about 3 cm (1¼ in.) long on the inside of the crown; these will probably be low enough to be covered by the petersham (make sure you move this out of the way).

10. Cut a narrow strip from the acetate sheet and arrange into a simple bow, making a stitch in the centre and wrapping tightly over and over, finishing with two stitches to secure the wrapped threads.

11. Use small stab stitches again to attach the bow to the hat, once more taking care to hold the petersham ribbon out of the way so the stitches are concealed behind it, rather than going through it.

12. The finished hat.

leather beret

WHAT YOU WILL NEED

- Black snakeskin embossed leather – 1 small skin, or large pieces from a skin
- 0.5 m (19½ in.) lining fabric
- Matching threads
- Petersham head fitting
- Sewing machine
- Beret pattern pieces (see page 135)

The beret is enduring and often iconic. This is a seamed, two-piece version of the classic beret normally formed in one piece from knitted or felted wool. The snakeskin-embossed leather brings a modern and sophisticated edge, but the beret also works well in soft woven fabrics.

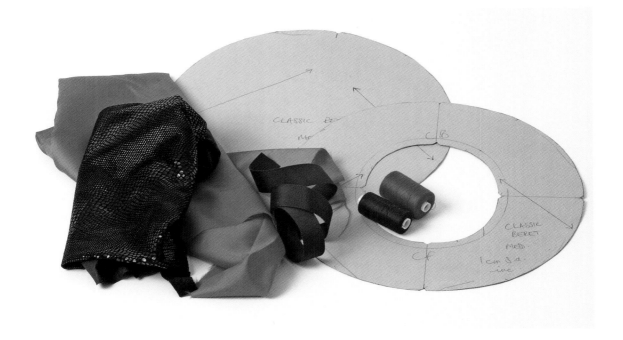

1. Before cutting out the pattern pieces, check the leather for any flaws that should be avoided. Hold it up to the light to check for any tiny holes that may not be visible otherwise, and circle these in biro or chalk on the back. Other than that, the pattern pieces can be laid in any direction.

2. The pattern pieces for the lining should be laid out with the grain lines parallel to the straight grain of the fabric.

2

3. Pin the two pieces together around the outside edge, matching notches first. For this hat, it is the tip that must be eased onto the sideband; the latter can be stretched slightly to fit as they are pinned.

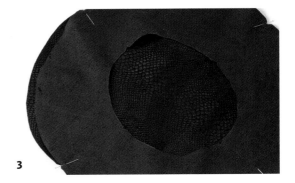

3

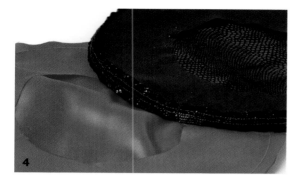

4

5

4. After stitching, open the seams and topstitch each side. This will give a more rounded effect than topstitching with the seam allowance on one side of the seam. Trim the excess seam allowance afterwards.

5. Insert the lining, and stitch together about 0.7 cm ($^5/_{16}$ in.) from the head-fitting edge.

6. Pin the petersham head-fitting in place and stitch very close to the lower edge of the petersham, removing each pin as the foot reaches it. Trim away the excess as far as the previous line of stitching, behind the petersham.

7. The finished hat.

6

7

fur-felt perching cap

WHAT YOU WILL NEED

- ▶ 1 fur-felt cone
- ▶ Patent leather remnant or approx. 30 cm if bought as a strip
- ▶ Matching threads
- ▶ 2 D-rings for trim
- ▶ Petersham head fitting
- ▶ Hat elastic
- ▶ Pillbox block
- ▶ Peak pattern piece (see page 131)
- ▶ Iron, bowl of water and pressing cloth
- ▶ Brush

A cheeky but feminine take on a military cap, this perches coquettishly on the side of the head. The peak is made using the same pattern piece as for the corduroy cap.

Tools and equipment.

1

2

1. The cheetah print on this melusine-felt hood is partly double-sided and so is ideal for making a hat with a small brim or, in this case, a visor. Turn the hood inside out and stiffen just the plain part of the felt; leave to dry completely.

2. This top part of the hood is just the right size to form the crown part of the cap and can be cut away from the printed part either before blocking or afterwards. Melusine felt can be blocked either using steam from a kettle or steamer, or by using a damp cloth and hot iron. The pile should be brushed after blocking. When dry, mark the CF and CB with chalk or with tie tacks before removing from the block.

3. Use the double-sided part of the felt now for the peak: this doesn't need to be blocked but can be cut out after drawing around the peak pattern piece. If necessary, smooth out the felt first by pressing through a damp cloth.

4. After cutting out, the outside edge must be turned and pressed: working on a small section at a time, fold the edge over about 0.5 cm (about $^1/_4$ in.) and iron through a damp cloth. Then hold in place while it dries/cools, before moving on to the next section.

5. This now needs to be stitched in place, either by hand (see page 37) or by machine. If machining, pull out the pile of the fur felt afterwards, using a needle or pin with a brushing action next to the stitches; this causes them to disappear. The felt can then be brushed smooth.

6. Pin the peak in place onto the crown, matching CF marks. This is stitched using backstitch to make it very secure.

7. Next, attach the hat elastic at each side, and the petersham ribbon.

Note: The petersham should be cut to fit the crown rather than the actual head size, as this crown is much smaller than most heads. The cap will be held in place with the elastic.

8. Cut a strip of patent leather for the front half of the cap; the ends can be pointed or cut straight. Use a ruler to ensure a perfect straight edge. After cutting, if the edge of the leather is discoloured, simply go over it with a black marker pen.

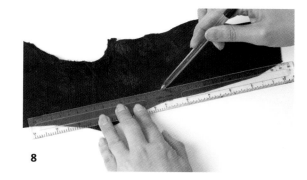

8

9

10

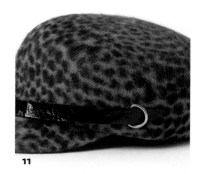

11

9. Arrange the leather strip in place against the front of the cap, and mark with pins where the D-rings should be attached (i.e. about 2 cm (³/₄ in.) in from each end of the leather strip). Remove the leather and secure each D-ring by stitching over the base (straight part).

10. Then replace the leather, threading each end through the D-rings, and stitch this in place about 1 cm (³/₈ in.) from the base of each D-ring.

11. These stitches will be covered up by the curved part of the D-rings when moved into position to face backwards.

12. The finished hat.

12

nylon-crin veil

WHAT YOU WILL NEED

▸ Approx. 2 m (78 in.) black crin, 2.5 cm (1 in.) wide
▸ Purchased plastic Alice band, 1.5 cm (⅝ in.) wide
▸ Bias strip of black satin approx. 5 x 37 cm (2 x 14½ in.)
▸ Matching thread

Enigmatic and alluring yet ultramodern, this is a cross between a veil and a mask. The nylon-crin strips here are 2.5 cm (1 in.) in width, but it is also widely available in 15 cm (6 in.) width. This has been a standard material for hats for some time – it was out of fashion for a while but currently seems to be enjoying a resurgence.

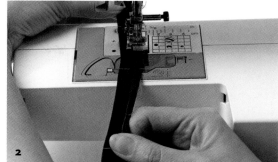

1

1. The bias strip of satin is stitched into a wide rouleau to fit tightly around the hairband: fold it in half lengthways, right sides together, and pin to hold. A stitching line can be marked, if required: measure from the folded edge 1.7 cm ($^{11}/_{16}$ in.) (for a hair band 1.5 cm/$^5/_8$ in. in width) and mark a line in chalk.

2. When stitching this on the machine, pull the satin strip as much as it will go. This is essential to allow elasticity, otherwise when it is stretched onto the hairband the stitches will break. Although it will appear to become too narrow while stretched, it will revert to the correct width when slack again.

3. Use a large safety pin to pull one end through the rouleau so the right side emerges.

4. Insert the hairband into the satin rouleau; try to keep the seam allowance inside the satin to lie in one direction only, with the seam remaining on the inside of the band.

5. At one end of the band, fold in about 0.5 cm ($^1/_4$ in.) of satin and slip-stitch the folded ends together. The hairband is a little narrower at the ends, so the satin will need to be gathered in slightly as it is slip-stitched.

3

4

5

6

7

8

9

6. When one end is secure, the satin can be stretched very tight and pinned to hold it in place at the other end, while the excess is trimmed away (leave about 0.5 cm ($^1/_4$ in.) for turning in again here). This end can now be slip-stitched in the same way. Prepare needle and thread before removing the pin so that the ends can be folded in very quickly and the first stitch made before the satin shrinks back.

7. Start arranging the crin onto the satin band; the first end is folded in 1 cm ($^3/_8$ in.) and pinned to the satin on one side. Take the crin across and pin in place on the other side, but lower down on the band. The length of the crin between the sides of the band should be about 35 cm (13 $^3/_4$ in.). This will prevent the crin irritating the face when worn. The crin can now simply be folded back on itself ready to form the next layer. Repeat this so that there are five strips criss-crossing between the sides of the hairband. This veil, or mask, works best if the crin strips are arranged quite randomly; each layer can vary slightly in length (remembering not to go much lower than the 35 cm/13 $^3/_4$ in.) and can be crossed under as well as over previous layers. Keep checking in the mirror to see the effect, and make adjustments as necessary.

8. Stitch the crin along each side of the satin band, using a diagonal stitch to create a zigzag effect. This will be very secure and, although relatively visible, is quite an attractive stitch.

9. The finished mask/veil.

gallery – attitude

ABOVE This veiled headband is a little more conventional than the crin mask/veil, but still creates a strong impact. It has been made in a similar way to the bridal headdress seen on page 111 , but with a black felt abstract bow in place of beads, providing a more substantial accompaniment to the dramatic veil.

ABOVE RIGHT Windswept® FLATcap in wool tweed. This very new and modern version of the iconic English flat cap has lots of attitude and works particularly well in traditional British fabrics.

RIGHT This headpiece is made from marabou feathers that have been partly trapped and laminated with sheer nylon fabric, to give a slightly edgier feel than the more conventional softness of pure marabou. From Suffragette City couture collection.

6 luxury

cossack hat

WHAT YOU WILL NEED

▶ 0.5 m (19½ in.) good-quality faux fur
▶ Small piece of toning wool/cashmere for tip
▶ Matching threads
▶ Sew-in interlining (stiff cotton or Vilene) for sideband
▶ Fusible cotton interlining for tip
▶ 0.5 m (19½ in.) satin lining
▶ Petersham head fitting
▶ Flared sideband and matching tip pattern pieces (see page 128)
▶ Sewing machine

An enduring style, evocative yet practical. This hat has a contrasting tip in wool/cashmere, but is even more luxurious when made entirely in the fur fabric.

1

2

First, iron the fusible cotton to the back of the wool/cashmere and leave this to cool. Next, cut out the sideband in the stiff cotton and the fur fabric separately, with the CF on the bias each time.

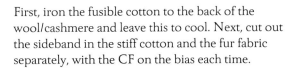

1. When cutting the fur fabric, allow the scissors to cut only through the backing part of the fabric; use just the tips of the scissors for this.

2. The fur part is then torn away; this means that the maximum amount of fur is left to work with, ensuring a full, luxurious effect, and concealing seams.

3

3. Attach the interlining to the fur sideband by large diagonal tacking stitches, catching just the backing part of the fur fabric. The tip can also now be cut out of the wool/cashmere, remembering that this must also be cut on the bias.

4. Pin the CB seam of the sideband, pushing all the fur inside. Then machine-stitch (but no topstitching for this hat). Afterwards, if necessary, fur can be pulled out from the seam on the right side with a needle, to further conceal the seam.

4

5. The sideband is now stitched to the tip – pin first, and machine over the pins. In this case, it isn't necessary to cut tabs along the sideband edge as the fabric is very flexible. The seam allowance can be trimmed down slightly afterwards.

5

6

6. Attach the petersham ribbon – again, pin it in place first before machining. While pinning the petersham, push the fur to the outside.

7. The quilted satin lining is made from the same pattern, but remember to make slightly larger seam allowances.

8. The lining for this hat has been slip-stitched in place behind the petersham head fitting. First, check how the lining fits inside – it might need to be trimmed away a little, leaving 1 cm ($^3/_8$ in.) to fold in. Pin first, then slip-stitch in place behind the petersham.

9. The finished hat.

7

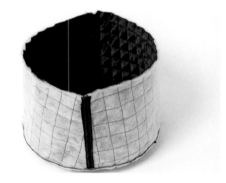

8

9

silk headpiece

WHAT YOU WILL NEED

- One 25 x 25 cm (10 x 10 in.) square of each:
  Buckram
  Fusible domette
  Silk taffeta
  Silk dupion for lining
- Matching thread
- Cotton thread for base
- Firm millinery wire
- Bias strip of tarlatan
- Hat elastic
- One long pheasant feather
- Assorted beads
- Dome crown block
- Iron
- Soap

This is a statement hat, yet has a subtlety, especially when worn over dark hair. The encrusted crystals provide a sparkling contrast to the pheasant feather, while the silk is sleek and glossy.

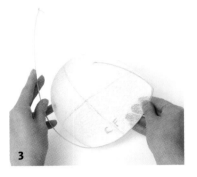

1. First make the firm base. Briefly immerse the buckram in water, then fold it up and place it in an airtight plastic bag for a few minutes. This will allow the buckram to absorb the water and will make it soft and pliable for blocking. It will, however, also make it very messy, so a plastic apron is recommended! Place the buckram onto the top part of the block. First secure the straight-grain edges (pin one side, then the opposite side). Make sure that the pins are pointing upwards as they enter the block. Once the straight edges are secure, pull each of the corners and pin these. There is a lot of elasticity in the buckram when wet; make sure that it is pulled as tightly as possible so that there is no movement or slackness left.

2. When dry (several hours later), draw the required shape of the headpiece and mark the CF, CB and two side points. In this case, the shape is an oval with a point slightly to one side of the centre front; this will provide a focal point for the draping of the silk and the position of the feather later on. Now the base can be removed from the block; cut out, using paper-cutting scissors (buckram will blunt good dressmaking scissors). Transfer the markings onto the underside of the base.

3. Cut a length of firm millinery wire to fit the circumference of the buckram base with about 6 cm (2 in.) overlap added. The wire will sit on the inside edge of the buckram and will need to be shaped gently by hand to match the concave curve of the buckram. Stitch using blanket stitch, ensuring that the ends of the wire are secured tightly. In this case it is not necessary to make a bound join for the ends of the wire; extra stitches over the ends will be enough to keep them in place.

4. Take the bias strip of tarlatan and fold in half lengthways, pulling it to its maximum. Place it over the wire and stitch a running stitch with cotton thread. Don't fold in any of the edges; simply overlap the ends by about 1 cm ($^3/_8$ in.) and cut away the excess tarlatan.

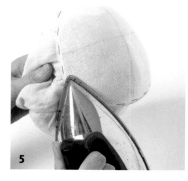

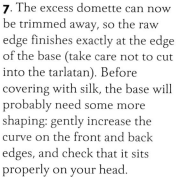

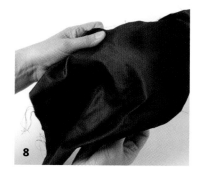

5. The tarlatan must now be ironed smooth, on the top side only. Use a pad behind the buckram shape to support it and to protect your hand. Dab water with your fingertips over the tarlatan edge and press, using only the very tip of the iron. Soap can also be rubbed over this join, to provide a waxy surface; iron again over this to achieve a very smooth finish.

6. Finally, to give a softer, slightly cushioned base for the silk, fusible domette is used as an interlining. Place it onto the buckram, pinning the straight-grain edges close to the

circumference so that it lies taut. Start to iron the domette in the centre, removing the pins once it is secure there. Start to iron outwards, where the pins had been, and pull the corners of the domette so it is smooth all over.

7. The excess domette can now be trimmed away, so the raw edge finishes exactly at the edge of the base (take care not to cut into the tarlatan). Before covering with silk, the base will probably need some more shaping: gently increase the curve on the front and back edges, and check that it sits properly on your head.

8. Place the silk taffeta onto the base, pulling it smooth around the front, back and left side. The excess fabric will be taken up as folds on the right side, next to the pointed part of the base.

9. Secure the silk by pinning it to the tarlatan on the inside.

10. Returning to the right side, arrange the folds, keeping it quite random; this part will also need to be pinned in place in the same way.

11. Stitch the silk to the tarlatan on the inside of the base, removing each pin as you reach it, and making sure that the silk remains smooth and taut where required. This stitch is similar to backstitch but is slightly diagonal, and so covers a slightly bigger surface area, holding the fabric more effectively and trapping any small pleats. After stitching, the excess silk is trimmed away (but don't discard yet) and the elastic is attached at each side. Before doing this, however, try the headpiece on to confirm that this is how you would like to position it on the head. It isn't necessary to come through to the right side when stitching the elastic – it should be held securely just on the silk/tarlatan edge on the underside.

12. Clean away any fluff from the base of the feather so that there is about 5 cm (2 in.) of clear spine at the base. Next, cut a bias piece from the corner of the excess silk and fold in half lengthways. This is now stitched to the spine. Wrap the folded silk tightly around the rest of the spine and stitch securely at the bottom. It is not necessary to fold in the raw edge as this will be covered by the beads.

13. Start to stitch the large crystals to the silk first, spacing them randomly, then add smaller beads and crystals to fill in between. The end of the spine should become quite encrusted, with hardly any visible gaps, but can gradually thin out towards the top of the bound silk.

14. Arrange the beaded feather in place on the silk headpiece, checking the position in the mirror before stitching. Use stab stitches to go right through the silk-bound spine to the inside of the buckram base until it is secure, with no movement. It will be easy to conceal stitches

amongst the beading. The lower part of the feather can also be secured to the base – stitch through the spine in three places, and go right through to the inside of the base each time.

15. To line the inside, carefully place the headpiece upside down, and place the silk dupion inside. Make sure it fits as closely to the buckram as possible. This will also require some pleating to accommodate the excess fabric. Pin in place, through the silk taffeta/tarlatan edge, and carefully trim away the dupion so there is about 1 cm ($^3/_8$ in.) seam allowance all around. Then fold in this seam allowance, removing and replacing each pin.

16. The lining can now be slip-stitched onto the silk taffeta edge. The silk dupion as a lining fabric continues the note of luxury, but is also a practical choice, as the texture helps allow the headpiece to stay in place.

17. The finished hat.

feather headpiece

WHAT YOU WILL NEED

- ▶ 0.2 m (8 in.) sinamay
- ▶ Approx. 20 cm (8 in.) hackle feather strip (two sizes if possible)
- ▶ Matching thread
- ▶ Large glass button or crystal
- ▶ Millinery wire
- ▶ Dome crown block
- ▶ Straw varnish
- ▶ Glue
- ▶ Hat elastic

This headpiece offers an accessible luxury. It is very easy to wear and actually works equally well with formal dress or jeans – the sort of hat that can be slipped on to take an outfit from day to evening, in the way a piece of jewellery might.

1. Block the three layers of sinamay on the dome crown block; the straight edges should be secured first, followed by the corners. Water-based stiffener can be applied after blocking, if required. When almost dry, iron over the sinamay; this will give a smooth finish and will allow the layers to adhere to each other. Draw in the required shape, allowing 1 cm (³⁄₈ in.) all around for a rolled edge. This is a similar shape to the silk headpiece but with the point at one end of the oval rather than to the side. It is also slightly smaller, although the finished hat will be about the same size as the silk one, as the feathers will extend over the edge all around.

2. Measure and cut the required length of wire (allowing about 6 cm/2³⁄₈ in. overlap). The wire should be shaped to fit the sinamay base and should be very slightly shorter than the actual measurement, so that the shape doesn't become flattened when the wire is attached. Here, the ends have been joined before rolling the sinamay edge, but this could be left until the last minute, just before rolling the back section. This allows some flexibility in how curved the shape becomes – the shorter the wire, the more curved the shape; the longer the wire, the flatter the shape becomes. Just like the rolled edge on the classic straw hat, the edge of the sinamay should be varnished and allowed to nearly dry, then rolled (see classic straw hat, page 105). This size of headpiece should be completed in two sections; if the whole circumference is varnished, it is likely that the varnish will have dried too much before reaching the end.

3. Prepare the hackle feathers: these have been purchased on a string, which makes it quick and easy to remove the fluffy part at the base of each feather. Simply cut through the whole bunch about 2 cm (³⁄₄ in.) from the ends that are attached to the string. There are two sizes of feather here, which gives a varied effect, but it would also work with just one size.

4. The feathers will be attached to the base in roughly circular layers, working from the outside inwards. It is a good idea to mark with a tie tack the finishing point on the base, somewhere in the centre. In this case, it is slightly nearer the rounded end so that the hat doesn't look bottom-heavy (it will be worn with the pointed end at the top and the rounded end at the bottom). This will also be the point at which the glass button or bead will be stitched.

Apply some glue around the edge of the sinamay base, and place some of the larger feathers along here, side by side and very close together. Work on a section at a time so that the glue doesn't dry before you place each feather.

5. When the first row is complete, go over it again, so that there is double the number of feathers here. The next row should be glued directly above the first row (this time use the smaller feathers, so that they finish only just over the rolled sinamay edge). Then continue with more layers, alternating between the large and the small (so that the layers are gradual, but without any bulk). If there is only one size of feather to work with, cut some of them shorter.

6. The rounded end of the base will need extra layers incorporated, as there is more surface area to fill here.

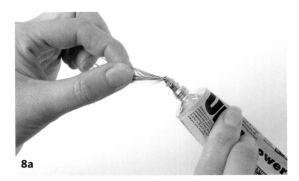

7. Once the base is completely covered, check once again on how it will sit on the head, before attaching the elastic. The ends of the elastic can be discreetly stitched to the rolled edge of the sinamay.

8. Stitch the glass button in place (remove the tie tack first). Now extra (small) feathers can be inserted around the button **(8b)**, this time apply the glue to each feather individually **(8a)**.

9. The finished hat.

9

gallery – luxury

ABOVE LEFT The chartreuse colour of this soft velour perching hat contributes to the feeling of luxury, and is accentuated by the rich purple of the ribboning. From Empire Lines couture collection.

ABOVE This hairband is made from velour felt pieces arranged onto a wire hairband. From Empire Lines couture collection.

LEFT This feathered hairband is a signature piece by Yasmin Rizvi. PHOTO: CAROLINE MARKS

7 occasion

sinamay pillbox

WHAT YOU WILL NEED

- ▶ 2 m (78 in.) sinamay (main colour)
- ▶ Two contrasting colours of sinamay – one full-length bias strip of each, approx. 15 cm (6 in.) wide
- ▶ Matching threads
- ▶ Firm millinery wire
- ▶ Petersham head fitting
- ▶ Hat elastic
- ▶ Dome crown block
- ▶ Iron
- ▶ Water spray
- ▶ Glue

The shape of this pillbox is quite strong but is softened by the exuberant flower trimming, giving it a very feminine look. The lightness of the sinamay makes it extremely comfortable for wearing all day.

1. Cut three squares of sinamay for the tip, about 25 cm (10 in.) square. Place together, spray with water and iron them together, turning them over to iron both sides. This will make the fabric easier to handle, when blocking. The dome crown block is turned upside down and covered with a plastic bag or cling film. Spray the sinamay squares with water and place them onto the block so that the bias runs from end to end and side to side. Start by blocking the straight grain edges first, as these will not stretch, followed by the corners, which will stretch a lot (each layer can be pulled separately if necessary). If the sinamay starts to dry as you work, simply respray with water.

2. The pins should be inserted at least 2 cm ($^3/_4$ in.) down from the top edge, with the points directed upwards. Leave this to dry. If the sinamay is particularly soft, water-based stiffener can be applied. When almost dry, iron directly on the sinamay, to ensure the layers adhere well and give a crisp finish. Finally, don't forget to mark CF and CB in chalk, pencil or as tie tacks, on the edge of the tip.

3. Once the tip has been removed, the sideband can be blocked. Cut one complete bias strip and half a bias strip, each about 15 cm (6 in.) wide. The block should remain upside down for now. Starting at one end (secure here with a pin), spray with water and pull the complete bias strip around the block, wrapping it around twice and finishing back at the starting point. Here, any excess should be trimmed away, leaving just a small overlap. The sinamay should fit snugly without being tight.

4. The half bias strip will form the third and final layer: again starting at the same point, spray with water and pull this strip around the block in the same way, this time wrapping around just once. Overlap slightly and this time fold in the final end to conceal the raw edge (trim away any excess; 2 cm ($^3/_4$ in.) is plenty to be folded in). All

1

2

3

4

three layers can now be pinned in place on the flat base of the block, with drawing pins.

5. The block can now be placed the right way up (with the flat edge on the table top). Pull the sinamay upwards to fit the curve of the block, and secure along this edge with straight pins.

6. This pillbox is higher at the back, sloping down to a very short CF. For this reason, the join in the sideband will sit at the front end rather than the back, as this will be the more discreet option. Therefore, the join in the sinamay denotes the CF (if it doesn't sit exactly on the CF of the block, use pencil or chalk to mark the actual CF on the sinamay). At the opposite end, mark the CB, again on the flat part of the sinamay. Returning to the CF/join, measure 3 cm (1¼ in.) up from the base and mark with tailors chalk or pencil. At the CB, measure up 10 cm (4 in.) and mark. From here, draw a gently curving line in each direction to meet the mark at the front. Remove from the block and cut along this line.

7. This cut edge will be the bottom edge of the pillbox and will be folded in to form the head fitting. It is important that it doesn't stretch, so a wire should be fitted along here. Place a pin at the CB and measure around the inside, 1 cm (³/₈ in.) from the edge – this is the approximate measurement – plus 7 cm (2³/₄ in.) overlap for the wire.

8. Pin the wire in place 1 cm (³/₈ in.) from the edge; for now the ends are joined together temporarily with Sellotape to allow for adjustment. The wire should not be pushing the sinamay outwards at all; if it is, shorten the wire slightly. In fact, it is a good idea to make the wire slightly shorter than the sinamay measurement, so that the sinamay has to be eased onto the wire, creating a slightly more exaggerated curve, and a smaller head fitting. Once you are happy with the fit, the ends of the wire can be joined and the wire stitched in place; stitch over the wire, going

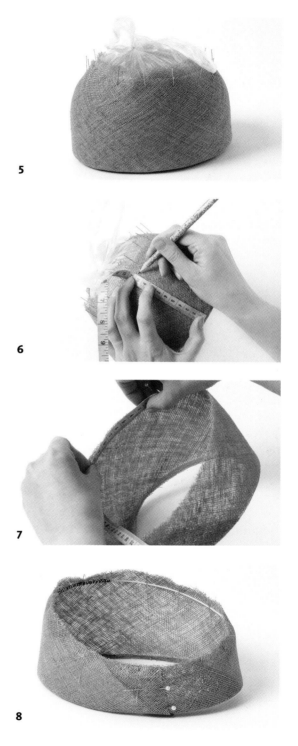

5

6

7

8

forward up to 1 cm ($^3/_8$ in.), then make another
stitch in the same place, before going forward
again. Each time, come through to the right side
with very small stitches; these should be almost
invisible against the texture of the sinamay.

9. Now work on the other edge of the sideband.
Trim away the excess sinamay so that there is no
more than a 1 cm ($^3/_8$ in.) edge. Using just the
very tip of the iron (dab a little water on the
sinamay edge first), press this edge flat against the
inside of the sideband. This will very slightly
stretch the edge, which is fine in this case, as the
tip needs to fit inside the sideband along here.
The tip should also be trimmed down so that the
edge is about 1 cm ($^3/_8$ in.) deep. The tip and
sideband are now ready to be attached.

10. Insert the tip into the sideband, matching CF
and CB, and pin. Stitch together, using a stab
stitch which is tiny on the outside and about
0.5 cm (about $^1/_4$ in.) apart on the inside.

11. Fold the head-fitting edge over the wire,
pressing with your fingertips (no need to iron).
Attach the hat elastic, one end at each side of the
sideband.

12. The petersham head fitting can now also be
attached.

Note: The petersham should be cut to fit the
pillbox rather than the actual head size, as the hat
will be held in place with elastic and will fit most
head sizes.

9

10

11

12

13a

13b

13. To make the flowers for the trimming, start by cutting another bias strip of the main colour sinamay, about 15 cm (6 in.) wide, to match the two contrast colours. **(13a)** Cut each strip into five smaller pieces – the lengths should vary from about 15 cm (6 in.) to about 25 cm (10 in.). Each piece is tapered into a basic petal shape **(13b)**.

14

14. The edges on each petal are turned in and ironed; fold over each side about 0.5 cm ($^1/_4$ in.) and iron flat, allowing the sinamay to stretch slightly along its length as you iron – this will help keep the turning very tiny. At the top, one side should simply be folded over the other.

15

15. Repeat the process, so there is a double fold for each side, on each petal. This time, spray with a little water before ironing till dry. This reactivates the stiffener in the sinamay so that it works like a glue to keep the folded edges permanently in place.

16. The top of each petal should have ends sticking out. Before removing these, put a little glue at the point where the folded edges cross over right at the tip, press together and allow to dry.

16

17

18

17. The ends can now be cut away, leaving crisp, pointed ends. Each petal can also now be curled slightly around the fingers to give a natural, flowing appearance.

18. Take a combination of colours in the smaller and medium-size petals and arrange into a bunch of about five or six, stitching them together at their bases. Adding one at a time, gather in each petal tightly as you stitch, so that the end of the bunch is small and neat. Then repeat this with the remaining small/medium-size petals. (Here, they are divided into four and six but could equally be five in each.) Finally, three of the longest petals are joined together, while two are left aside for now.

19

19. The first bunch is stitched onto the edge of the tip at the right-hand side of the hat.

20. The second bunch is stitched onto the sideband just below the first. Arrange and stitch one or two of these petals to cover and hide the ends of the first bunch.

20

21. Finally, the larger bunch is added, just next to the previous bunch. One of these petals is curled around to the front of the hat and stitched to cover the seam at the CF. The two remaining petals are now stitched over the ends and curled back on themselves to cover all the raw ends and the stitching.

22. The finished hat.

21

22

sinamay headpiece

WHAT YOU WILL NEED

- ▶ 1 full-length bias strip of sinamay about 15 cm (6 in.) wide
- ▶ Matching thread
- ▶ Metal or plastic comb
- ▶ Stripped coque feathers
- ▶ Water spray
- ▶ Glue

A very simple-to-make and easy-to-wear headpiece that can be worn from day into evening.

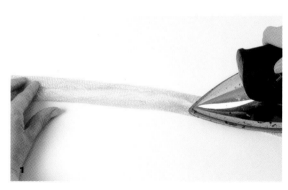

1. Stretch out the sinamay strip along its length; this will make it more flexible. As a result, it will also become thinner than the original 15 cm (6 in.). Fold in the two long edges so that they meet, (but don't overlap) in the centre; press these in place with a hot iron.

2. Fold in half again along the length and iron again, this time spraying with water first. Iron just a section at a time so that each section can be manipulated around your fingers into a spiral while it is still warm and flexible. This will give it a more natural and elegant appearance.

3

3. Arrange the curled rouleau into several, random loops, keeping the two ends free, and pin in place.

4. Stab-stitch the loops together and remove the pins. Make sure that the stitches are very tiny in any places likely to be visible. Sinamay is an ideal material for hiding stitches, as they can run in line with the woven strands.

5. The sinamay ends that were left free might need to be trimmed down; ideally the lengths should be slightly different. Fold in the edges on each end and stitch them closed using a small, neat overstitch.

6. This headpiece has a comb as a way of securing it into the hair. An alternative could be a wired headband (as shown on the bridal headdress). Before attaching the comb, check how the loops look on your head and decide where the front should be.

The comb should be attached using double thread: hold the comb nearly at a right angle to the base of the sinamay loops while stitching between each tooth. This will allow some flexibility to the comb, making it easier to secure in the hair.

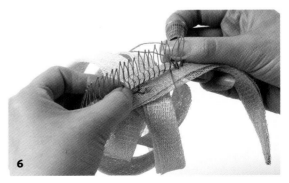

7

8a

8b

7. The feathers used here are stripped coque in two toning shades of blue. The ends have been shaped to give a more elegant appearance. To achieve this effect, use only very sharp scissors. Make sure that the fronds are lying smoothly and cut from the top downwards on each side.

8. The most efficient way to attach individual feathers like these is to use glue. **(8a)** In this case, pairs or groups of three have been inserted between layers of the sinamay loops at even distances around the whole piece. **(8b)** It is a good idea to keep checking the appearance in the mirror as you work; it is easy to move the feathers around while the glue is fresh. To give a more abundant look to the headpiece, many more feathers could be used. In this case, there are about 15.

9. The finished headpiece.

9

classic straw hat

WHAT YOU WILL NEED

- ▸ 1 parasisal straw capeline
- ▸ Matching thread
- ▸ Bias strip of buckram
- ▸ Firm millinery wire
- ▸ 0.5 m (19½ in.) silk dupion
- ▸ Silver buckle
- ▸ Petersham head fitting
- ▸ Dome crown block
- ▸ Large bell-shaped brim block with collar attached
- ▸ Straw stiffener

This hat has a timeless elegance. The basic shape can be dressed up with a more ornate trimming for a special occasion, or dressed down to be worn as a simple sun hat.

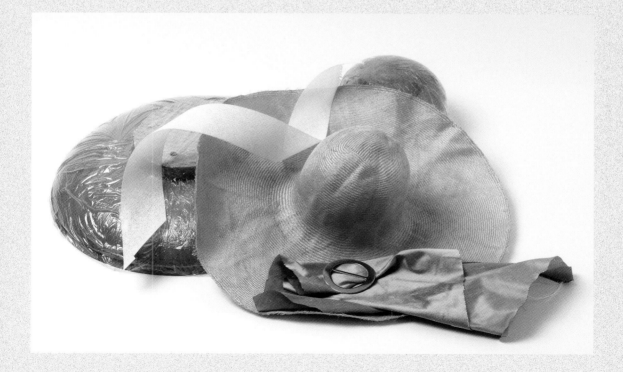

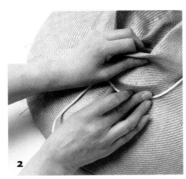

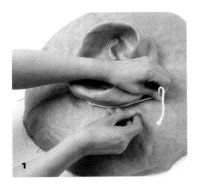

1. Each block should be covered with a plastic bag or cling film. The brim should be blocked first. Immerse the straw capeline in water, then place onto the brim block. Anchor it in position with pins around the outside edge so that it lays evenly all around, with an equal amount of selvedge to pin into. Pins can be about 15 cm (6 in.) apart; this is just to hold it in place while the head fitting is blocked securely around the collar of the block. Here, use a blocking cord, place the cord around the collar and thread the other end of the cord through the loop, pulling tightly. Secure the end of the cord to the collar with a pin.

2. The outer edge can now be blocked properly: place another, longer cord around the outer edge, just above the holding pins, and pull tightly again. Secure the end with a pin and remove the holding pins. Now return to the head fitting. Release the cord, pull the straw through again tighter still and replace the cord, pinning

securely again. Check that the straw is pulled as taut as possible with no movement left at all. If there is still some slackness left, pull again at the outer edge; if necessary remove the pin from the cord and pull this again, replacing the pin.

3. Cut away the crown part of the hood along the top edge of the collar, using a knife or pointed scissors. Dampen this straw again if necessary and place onto the crown block. Make sure that the cross in the centre of the hood remains central on the top of the crown block. Pin along the edge of the straw so that the pins point upwards as they enter the block.

3

4. When the straw is completely dry, both shapes can be varnished with straw stiffener while still on the block. Don't overload the brush with the varnish; it is better to apply two or three layers of stiffener sparingly each time rather than one layer very thickly. When the varnish is dry, CF and CB marks should also be pencilled onto both shapes before removal from the blocks.

5. The crown will need a buckram extension added. Firstly, find the shortest part of the straw and make a pencil mark 1 cm ($^3/_8$ in.) up from the edge of the straw. Measure down from this mark to the bottom of the block and use this same measurement to mark all around the crown. This will be the line at which the buckram extension will join the straw. Make sure that the CF and CB marks remain visible. Adding an extension means the height of the crown for the finished hat is not dependent on the height of the block. In this case, the buckram extension is 6 cm ($2^3/_8$ in.) in height, so the finished crown will be slightly taller than the block itself. As this part of the crown is straight all around the circumference, it is not necessary to block the buckram; a simple bias strip works well. (The length of the buckram should be the same as the circumference of the block, with overlap added.)

5

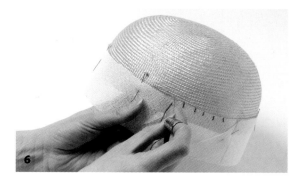

6

7

6. Starting at the CB, pin the buckram strip to the straw crown so the top edge of the buckram sits along the pencil line. Transfer the CF and CB marks onto the buckram sideband. The stitch for this is an overstitch about 0.5 cm (^{1}/$_4$ in.) deep and 1 cm (^{3}/$_8$ in.) long (diagonal) on the inside. This will ensure that the buckram cannot move. The buckram overlap should also be stitched in the same way.

7. The brim on this hat has a rolled edge, which gives a very clean, simple and couture look to the hat. Remove the brim from the block and trim away the selvedge. Place a pin at the CB as a starting point and measure the circumference, 0.75 cm (^{5}/$_16$ in.) from the underside edge. Cut a length of wire to this measurement, adding about 7 cm (2 ^{3}/$_4$ in.) for overlap.

8

8. The wire join should be made temporarily with Sellotape to allow for adjustments. Once the wire has been pinned in place (with the join at CB), it might need to be made slightly shorter than the original measurement to allow room for the straw to roll over and under the wire without stretching and flattening out the brim shape. The Sellotape can remain (before permanently joining the wire ends) until the last minute, before rolling the final section of the brim.

9a

9. To achieve a really finely rolled edge, it is best to apply extra varnish just to the edge, and to roll before the varnish dries and while the straw is still soft. For this reason, it is necessary to work on one section of the brim at a time: in this case, with quite a large brim, probably about a quarter of the circumference at a time, starting near the CB, to the left of the temporary join. Remove the pins from this first section, and brush on the varnish, leaving it for a short time: this period can vary depending on the temperature of the room in which you are working, but is likely to be no more than five minutes. In any case, once the straw is dry enough to handle but still soft and slightly tacky, fold the edge over no more than 0.5 cm (about ¹/₄ in.) **(a)**. Then turn this folded edge over the wire, whilst pushing the raw edge underneath the wire with your fingernails. Now apply a rolling action with the brim edge between your fingertips and thumbs to give a rounded rather than flat finish. **(b)** When the section is complete, go back over it to make it as tightly and neatly rolled as possible. By now, the straw will probably be much firmer as the varnish dries and hardens. Repeat the whole process for each of the remaining sections, finishing at the back (finish the join in the wire before rolling the final section). The edge shouldn't need to be stitched – the stiffener is enough to hold it in place permanently. If the stiffener was allowed to dry and/or the edge is rolled rather loosely, it should be stitched using a tiny stab stitch on each side.

10. The petersham head fitting is now attached, before joining the crown and brim.

11. Pin the crown onto the brim, moving the petersham out of the way so that the pins are behind it. The CF and CB marks on the sideband should line up exactly with those on the brim. The stitch here is a backstitch, close to the bottom edge; again, make sure that the stitches are behind the petersham and not through it.

12. The hat is now ready to be trimmed. First decide on the position for the focal point of the trim – i.e. where the silk pleats will cross over and where the buckle, in this case, will sit. (An

9b

10

11

12

HATS

13

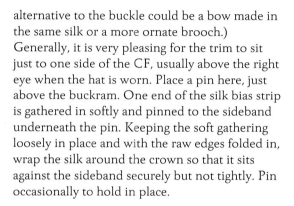

14

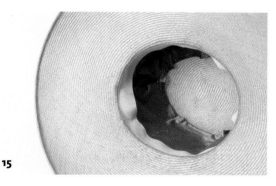

15

alternative to the buckle could be a bow made in the same silk or a more ornate brooch.) Generally, it is very pleasing for the trim to sit just to one side of the CF, usually above the right eye when the hat is worn. Place a pin here, just above the buckram. One end of the silk bias strip is gathered in softly and pinned to the sideband underneath the pin. Keeping the soft gathering loosely in place and with the raw edges folded in, wrap the silk around the crown so that it sits against the sideband securely but not tightly. Pin occasionally to hold in place.

13. On reaching the starting point, the silk is threaded through the buckle. Finish by tucking the end of the silk behind the pleating, along the lower edge of the crown, rearranging the pleating over it as necessary so that the raw edges are completely concealed. This will probably only require a couple of pins to keep in place before stitching.

14. As a general rule, make a stitch wherever there is a pin, with extra stitches as necessary. The stitches should be very tiny on the outside, sitting behind folds of silk. Inside, the stitches can be longer but ideally shouldn't exceed 3 cm ($1^1/_4$ in.). Again, when stitching at the base of the crown, remember to move the petersham out of the way. Make sure all pins are removed as you stitch. The top edge of the silk will probably need to be slip-stitched to the straw so that it can't move and thus reveal the buckram underneath.

15. It isn't usually necessary or desirable to line a straw hat, but in this case a simple half-lining has been inserted, to cover the buckram and stitching. (See linings, page 41)

16. The finished hat.

16

bridal headdress

- 35 cm (14 in.) fine nylon tulle
- Matching thread
- Firm millinery wire
- Assorted pearls

Made using traditional bridal tulle, the asymmetry gives this headdress a more modern look than it would have if placed directly in the centre front.

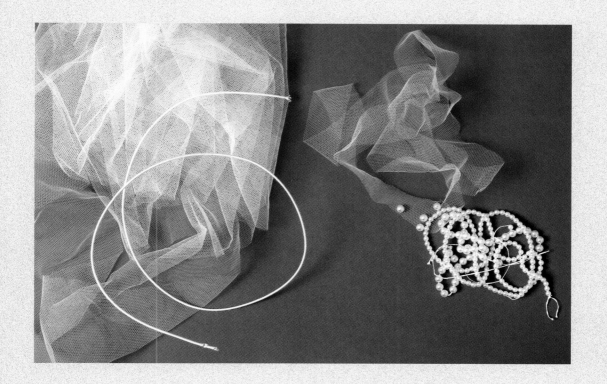

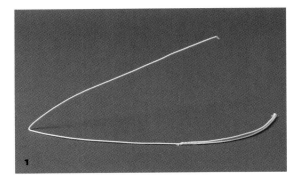

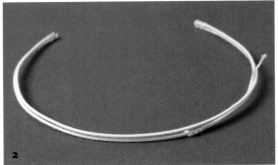

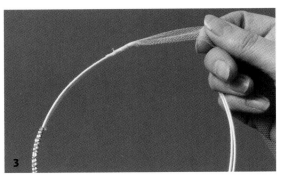

1. To make the wired headband, cut a length of wire 68 cm + 7 cm (26^3/$_4$ in. + 2^3/$_4$ in.) overlap = 75 cm (29^1/$_2$ in.), and make a bend about 15 cm from one end. From here, measure 34 cm (13^3/$_8$ in.) and make another bend.

2. Secure each of the two ends to the main part of the wire with Sellotape before binding all four layers of wire (see page 36). Shape the headband now so that it fits the head closely and so that it lies flat when placed on a surface.

3. Cut a strip of tulle about 1 m (39 in.) long and 3 cm (1^1/$_4$ in.) wide (not on the bias, as tulle is a type of net rather than a woven fabric and so doesn't have a bias; it is flexible in any direction). Dab a little glue on the wire band about 1cm (^{3}/$_8$ in.) from one end. Then place one end of the tulle strip here and start tightly wrapping it around the wire, work back to cover the end, and then forward again.

4. Continue wrapping the tulle tightly around the wire band. Try to keep tulle strip folded so that the folded edge covers the previous raw edge with each turn.

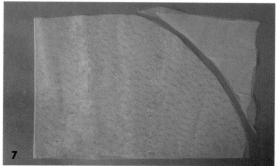

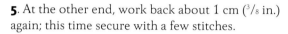

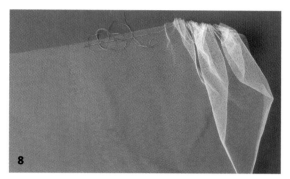

5. At the other end, work back about 1 cm (³/₈ in.) again; this time secure with a few stitches.

6. The wire headband will probably now need to be shaped again; try it on to check the fit and adjust as necessary.

7. Cut out a piece of tulle about 90 cm by 30 cm (36 in. by 12 in.). Cut away two of the corners, leaving curved edges.

8. Make a gathering stitch along the long curved edge.

9. Gather in the tulle until it measures about 10 cm (4 in.). Secure well with tight stitches.

10. The tulle veil can now be arranged with pins onto the headband. In this case, the veil is attached to the headband slightly to one side of the CF. Try on the headdress before stitching. The stitches should be diagonal, about 0.75 cm (⁵/₁₆ in.) long, yet will hardly be visible amongst the folds of the tulle.

11. Because the veil is sitting to one side, the lower edge of the tulle will of course hang lower at that side. Although the asymmetry works well in positioning the veil, the lower edge works better when lying evenly across the face and is in happy contrast with the asymmetry of the top part. So simply gather in more of the tulle at this lower side, pinning it and checking the appearance in the mirror. Then stitch in the same way along the original gathers. It will probably also need some stitches just in front of the band, through the folds of tulle alone. This more gathered-in effect also rounds off the veil on that side, thus framing the face and adding further contrast with the other side.

12. Finally, assorted sizes of pearls are stitched along the top edge – here they are arranged quite close together near the centre, thinning out randomly to each side.

13. The finished headdress.

gallery – occasion

ABOVE LEFT Straw is very versatile, and doesn't necessarily have to be used for a traditional crown and brim. Here a bright pink sisal straw has been sculpted, using steam, into a more abstract design. Sisal has a different weave to parasisal, and has a more textured appearance, giving it a slightly more casual look.

ABOVE CENTRE An exuberant but delicate bridal headdress by Edwina Ibbotson: tulle is liberally gathered in around handmade silk roses, with a scattering of crystals and beads individually stitched all over. PHOTO: JOANNE ALDRIDGE

ABOVE RIGHT A classic with a twist: this sinamay hat has been blocked on the same large brim block as the classic straw hat on page 105, but here the head fitting has been offset to create a dramatic asymmetric effect. The trim incorporates shredded, or frayed, sinamay with a curled ostrich quill, both of which have been highlighted by being partially sprayed with silver paint.

RIGHT Silver sinamay strips 'beehive' turban, from Empire Lines couture collection. This is made from very many flat sinamay rouleaux, which have been made in the same way as for the sinamay headpiece.

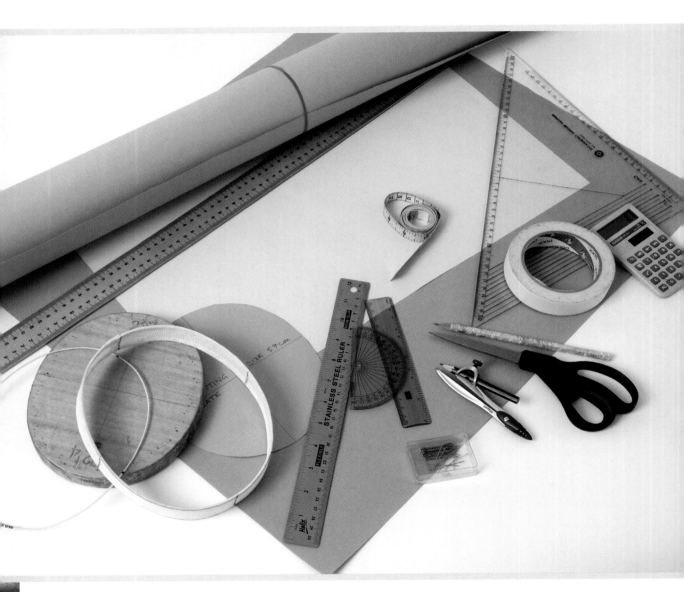

Pattern-cutting tools and equipment.

8 pattern-cutting

It should be noted that this chapter requires only a basic knowledge of maths, and while reasonably good measuring and line-drawing skills are required, this isn't about producing beautifully drafted technical drawings and patterns. The emphasis here is on achieving particular shapes to create interesting and exciting hats and caps, and hopefully gaining the knowledge and confidence to build on these basics and go ahead and experiment.

equipment

TOOLS AND EQUIPMENT FOR PATTERN-CUTTING

▶ Large sheets of plain paper – recycled sugar paper has been used here, in sheets of approx. 50 x 70 cm (19½ x 21½ in.)

▶ A4 paper also useful for smaller pattern pieces

▶ Card (optional) – for transferring paper patterns onto

▶ Set square(s) – available from outlets specialising in fashion workroom equipment – this really does make life easier for drawing right angles successfully!

▶ Basic protractor and compass set – these are readily available within basic geometry sets

▶ Pencil

▶ Ruler

▶ 1 m (39 in.) ruler – this is useful, but not essential for cutting hat patterns

▶ Tape measure

▶ Pins

▶ Sellotape/masking tape

▶ Paper-cutting scissors

▶ Calculator

▶ Head-fitting template

HEAD-FITTING TEMPLATE

An accurate head-fitting template of some description is very important, and there are several options for this. The simplest and most accurate option is a crown block, or a collar from a brim block in the required head size (make sure that it has clear and accurate CF and CB markings). If no block is available, then a wire head fitting could be made – this could be either simply a piece of wire joined together to form an oval or a buckram bias strip wired and bound with tarlatan on each edge (as used here). In either case, it is essential that the CF and CB (side points are also helpful) are marked accurately and that the template is a true oval in shape. Spend time checking measurements, and put it on to shape it to fit. The advantage here over using a block is that the head fitting will be, in theory at least, the exact shape for your head. Another alternative is to make a paper or card template – follow the instructions for an oval tip (see the two-piece pattern for the Cossack hat, page 128), using the head size for the circumference measurement.

pattern-cutting notes

1. Always work on patterns without seam allowance – this should be added right at the end, after all adjustments have been made. 1 cm ($^3/_8$ in.) is a good size for seam allowance, and has been used for the patterns here.

2. Always label patterns as soon as they are complete, to avoid any confusion between hats at a later date. This should include the name or style of hat and whether (and how much) seam allowance is added. It can also be helpful to write how many pieces should be cut in the fabric – for example, a brim will require two in the main fabric, while a tip and sideband will require just one of each, plus one of each in the lining fabric.

3. Grain lines are very important for ensuring that the pattern pieces are laid on the bias of the fabric. Place the central, diagonal line of the set square directly onto the CF line of the pattern, and draw lines against the two shorter edges of the set square. These are at right angles to each other, and the lines will be used to sit along the straight grains of the fabric, one in each direction. This will ensure that the CF will be on the true bias of the fabric.

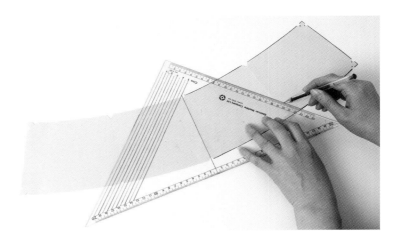

Here, grain lines are added to the tapered sideband, but every pattern piece should be treated in the same way.

4. It's never a good idea to 'save time' by not cutting notches on patterns – it inevitably leads to headaches trying to match seams correctly in fabric later on.

5. During the pattern-cutting stages, it's important to label CF and CB, especially early in the process when it is less obvious!

6. When cutting sideband and tip patterns for crowns, always make the tip slightly smaller in circumference (about 2 cm/$^3/_4$ in.) than the sideband. This will give a more professional finish.

7. It is a good idea to transfer each paper pattern onto a more hard-wearing card, especially if it is likely to become a favourite shape. It is also quicker and easier for drawing around the pattern onto fabric, without the need for pins. Use masking tape to secure the paper pattern on the card while drawing around it to avoid pinning into the card.

8. A note on π: this Greek letter (pronounced pye) equals 3.14, and is used here for drawing a circle for a tip pattern. But it is also used for working out traditional men's hat sizes: for example a head size of 22 in. (this only works in imperial) will be hat size 7 (22÷3.14=7).

pattern-cutting projects

The patterns featured here will make the project hats in question, if followed exactly. But of course once the basics are understood, there are endless possibilities for creating patterns for many different hats and caps other than the ones in this book.

Broadly speaking, crowns can be either square or round, with each having a different method for pattern-cutting. The rain hat and also the Cossack hat both have square crowns, whereas the corduroy cap is based on the round (or six-section) crown.

Both types require a very basic understanding of circles, so here is a reminder of a few basic principles.

THE FEATURED PATTERNS

1. Wide-brimmed hat with tapered sideband and round tip (rain hat, page 55)
2. Brimless hat with flared sideband and oval tip (Cossack hat, page 77)
3. Six-section cap with peak (corduroy cap, page 45)
4. Simple beret (leather beret, page 65)
5. Simple visor (straw visor, page 51)

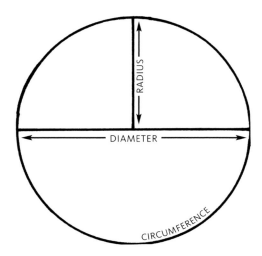

Circle showing circumference, diameter and radius.

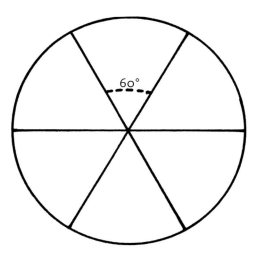

Circle divided into six, showing 60° angles.

The white/blue cotton cap here is an example of a square crown; this cap has been made from an old shirt, and it utilises various details from the shirt. The blue/gold cap has been made using the round cap (6-section) technique. It is fitted close to the head with quite a large, asymmetric peak as a contrast.

1. wide-brimmed hat

This two-piece crown pattern plus a wide brim pattern are used to make the coated cotton rain hat on page 55.

SIDEBAND

1

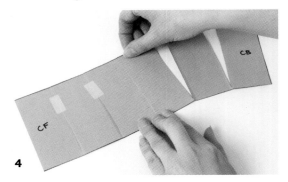

3

1. Begin with a half-pattern for a straight sideband, without seam allowance: this is a simple rectangle. In this case, the pattern is to fit a head size of 56.5 cm (22$\frac{1}{4}$ in.), plus 0.5 cm ($\frac{1}{4}$ in.) ease = 57 cm (22$\frac{1}{2}$ in.) (this is not a thick fabric and so requires very little ease). So the length of the half-pattern is 28.5cm (11$\frac{1}{4}$ in.) (half of 57); the height for this crown is 10 cm (4 in.). Make sure the ends of the rectangle are marked CF and CB.

3. Open out again and cut down each of the lines from the top edge, finishing just before reaching the lower edge.

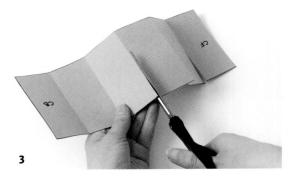

4

4. Cut five small pieces of Sellotape or masking tape ready to use for each section. Then close each section, overlapping by no more than 0.5 cm ($\frac{1}{4}$ in.) each time, and secure with a piece of the tape.

2

2. Divide the half-pattern into six equal sections by simply folding in half and then into three.

5. The crown for this hat has more of a slope inwards at the CF and CB than at the sides. So at each end, draw a new line 0.75 cm ($^5/_{16}$ in.) in at the top edge, going to nothing at the lower edge (shown here as broken lines). Cut along each of these lines completely.

6. Place the half-pattern onto a fresh piece of paper that has been folded in half. The new CF line should sit directly on the fold. Pin in place. Now the seam allowance can be added: measure 1 cm ($^3/_8$ in.) out from the edge of the half-pattern all around. Mark notches to indicate seam allowance at the CB, and half-notches at the CF fold.

7. The pattern can now be cut out along the seam allowance lines. Before removing the half-pattern, measure along the top edge, not including any seam allowance, either at the top edge or at the CB. This will provide the necessary measurement to begin working on the tip pattern. Hold the tape measure upright as this is easier and more precise for measuring a curve. This is half the pattern, so multiply by two to give the complete measurement for the circumference of the top of the sideband, and make a note of this for later. In this case, the total measurement is 46 cm (18 in.).

8. Remove the half-pattern and fold the new pattern piece in half to snip the notches for the side points. The original half-pattern can be either discarded or kept to be adapted for another pattern.

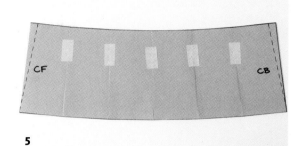

5

6

7

8

TIP

1. This is the top section of the two-piece crown; in this case it is simply a circle. Although it is probably more common for a tip to be slightly oval in shape, this sloping crown seems to work well with a circular tip. This is also the easier option – see the Cossack hat pattern for making an oval-shape tip.

The tip must be a perfect fit for the circumference of the sideband. In order to make the tip, it is therefore necessary to know the measurement of the sideband's top edge, or circumference, as it will be when joined with a seam (see step 7, tapered sideband). But there is one important point to remember: the circumference of the tip should be about 2 cm ($^3/_4$ in.) smaller than the circumference of the sideband. This will give a professional finish: when the pattern pieces are cut in fabric and stitched together, there will be a smooth, rounded effect at the seam where the side-band is eased onto the tip. So, returning to the measurement noted down earlier, subtract 2 cm ($^3/_4$ in.) from this. In this case, the sideband measures 46 cm (18 in.), so the equivalent tip measurement must be 44 cm ($17^1/_4$ in.).

2. In order to draw a circle, the length of the radius must be worked out by using the following simple formula:

Circumference divided by π = diameter
Note: π = 3.14

In this case, we know that the circumference for the tip has to be 44 cm ($17^1/_4$ in.) so: 44 ÷ 3.14 = 14.01

This means that the diameter of the tip will be 14 cm ($5^1/_2$ in.), and so the radius will be 7 cm ($2^3/_4$ in.)

3. Take a fresh sheet of paper, at least 10 cm (4 in.) square. Draw a large cross in the centre, using a set square to ensure perfect right angles.

4. Take the compass with pencil attached and set it to measure 7 cm ($2^3/_4$ in.). With the point of

the compass in the centre of the crossed lines, draw a circle.

5. The compass can now be reset to measure 8 cm ($3^1/_8$ in.), and a new larger circle added to give seam allowance. The pattern can now be cut out and labelled. Notches should be snipped at each of the four lines at the edge of the circle.

3

4

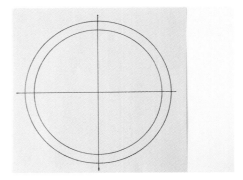

5

BRIM

1. To begin making the brim pattern, half of the head-fitting line must be drawn first using the head-fitting template. The CF and CB should sit exactly on the edge of a large, single piece of paper. If there is a side point marked on the template, this can also be marked.

2. From the head-fitting line, measure outwards the required length for the brim. In this case, the brim is longer at the front and sides than the back: 15 cm (6 in.) and 12 cm (4³/₄ in.) respectively. Measure out with a ruler from the head-fitting line 15 cm (6 in.) at the front and continue like this until the side point is reached. From this point onwards, each mark should be made at increments of about 0.5 cm (¹/₄ in.) less each time, with each mark being about 2–3 cm (³/₄–1¹/₄ in.) apart. Just before the CB is reached, the measurement should have reached 12 cm (4³/₄ in.).

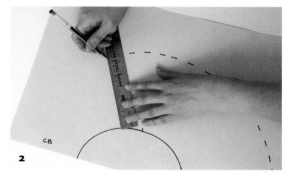

3. Join the marks together, keeping the curve as natural and clean as possible. It is much easier to draw concave curves such as this with your drawing hand inside the concave line rather than outside, and keeping the wrist flexible and relaxed. Turn the paper around as necessary to be able to do this.

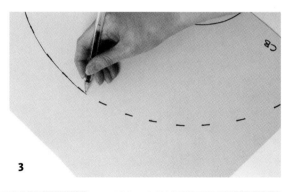

4. Cut out the brim shape and fold in half, then fold twice more. Because of its asymmetry, it won't line up completely, even at the head-fitting line, but here make sure it lines up as closely as possible.

4a

4b

4c

5. Reopen the brim: there should be eight sections clearly showing, four on either side of the side point.

6. These fold lines are now slashed, overlapped and taped, just like the sideband. But there is a difference here: to accommodate the oval shape of a head, it is necessary to overlap more at either side of the CF, but not actually at the CF itself as this would cause a flattening effect. And the side point requires a little less overlapping. For this particular hat, the actual amounts for each overlap are 3.5 cm (1³/₈ in.) at the slash nearest to the CF and also at the other end, close to the CB. The slash in the centre, which is the side point of the brim, overlaps by just 1 cm (³/₈ in.). Each of the other four overlaps measures 2 cm (³/₄ in.). This will ensure that the brim will turn up successfully at the front. For a brim with a gentler slope, not designed to turn up like this, a smaller overlap should be allowed for each slash. In fact, for a brim with a minimum of sloping, it wouldn't be necessary to have so many slashes/overlaps.

7. Pin the half-pattern onto a folded piece of paper, with the CF exactly on the fold. The slashing and overlapping cause the edges to lose the smooth line; this can be redrawn where necessary, shown here as broken lines.

8. Seam allowance can now be added.

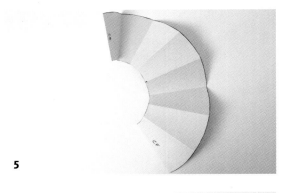

5

6

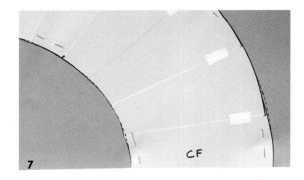

7

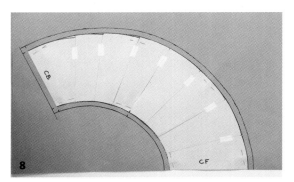

8

9. Cut out the pattern, including notches at CF and CB, and remove the half-pattern. This should be kept, for now, in case any adjustments are needed. While the new pattern piece is still folded at the CF, fold it again, so that it lies level at the head-fitting line and the CF is level with the CB (not the outer seam allowance line). The side point notches can now be snipped, at the head-fitting line as well as the outside edge.

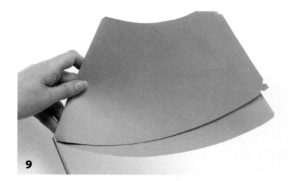

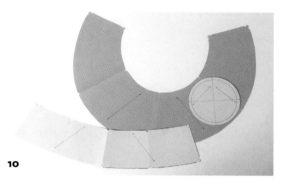

10. The three finished pattern pieces that make up the cotton rain hat are shown here. Grain lines have been added, and each pattern piece should also now be labelled: the style of hat and which part each piece relates to, how much seam allowance is added, and how many fabric pieces should be cut for each pattern piece.

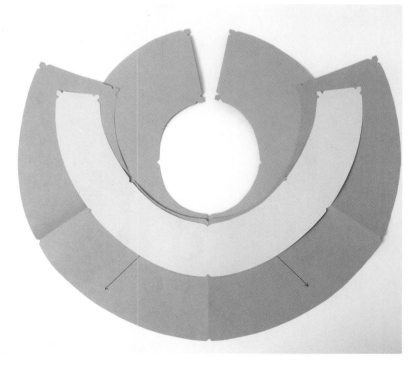

Here the brim pattern for the rain hat is sandwiched between two other brim patterns. The yellow card pattern underneath is for a brim that is almost flat, with just a gentle slope downwards to stop it sticking out from the head at a right angle. This would be most suitable for a stiff fabric, which would give it a slightly boaterish look, otherwise a soft fabric would make this shape of brim very floppy. The light-coloured brim pattern on top is for the trilby hat seen on page 137. Although much shorter, the shape is very similar, especially at the front. At the back, extra overlapping has been done so that the brim flips up at the back. As a quick way of recognising hat shapes from patterns, the steeper the angle on a brim, the more stretched open the head-fitting becomes.

2. brimless hat

This two-piece crown pattern is used to make the Cossack hat on page 77.

SIDEBAND

1. Start with a half-pattern straight sideband again. This time, the dimensions are 58 cm (22³/₄ in.) head size and 10.5 cm (4¹/₄ in.) height. So the half-pattern will measure 29 cm (11³/₈ in.) by 10.5 cm (4¹/₄ in.). This is to fit the same head size as previously, but here an extra 1cm ease has been added, to accommodate the thick fur fabric. Divide into six equal sections as for the tapered sideband on page 122.

2. Slash down each fold line again. This time each slash is opened slightly rather than overlapped. Start pinning onto a folded piece of paper, leaving about 2 mm (less than ¹/₈ in.) at the CF top edge, with the bottom edge of the CF sitting exactly on the fold.

3. Pin the remaining sections, opening each one about 2–3 mm (less than ¹/₈ in.). Add an extra 2 mm (less than ¹/₈ in.) at the CB top edge, going to nothing at the bottom edge. This hat has only a subtle flared shape at the top; for a more exaggerated shape, make each opening a little wider – up to 0.5 cm (about ¹/₄ in.). Seam allowance can now also be added.

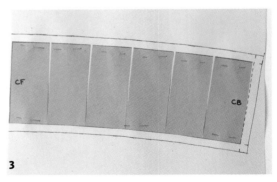

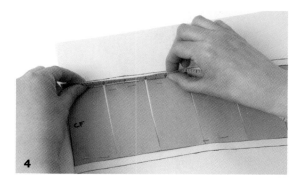

4

5

4. While the half-pattern is still in place, measure the top edge, not including seam allowance. The half-pattern measures 31.5 cm (12³/₈ in.), so the total sideband circumference will be 63 cm (24³/₄ in.). Just as with the tapered sideband, this measurement will be needed to cut the tip pattern.

5. Cut out the new full pattern, and remove the half-pattern. Fold the new pattern piece in half, matching CF to CB, and snip side-point notches.

TIP
As just noted, the sideband circumference for this hat is 63 cm (24³/₄ in.) so the tip circumference must measure 61 cm (24 in.).

To return to the simple formula: 61 ÷ 3.14 = 19.4

This means that the diameter will be 19.4 cm (7⁵/₈ in.) and the radius 9.7 cm (3¹³/₁₆ in.).

1. Draw a large cross on a piece of paper using a set square to ensure perfect right angles. From the centre of the cross, use the compass set to draw a circle with a radius of 9.7 cm (3¹³/₁₆in.).

2. This crown has an oval-shaped tip so the circle must be adjusted to become an oval. At the top of the circle start to draw a new arc about 0.75 cm (⁵/₁₆ in.) above the original. It should start at a right angle from the vertical line, before curving down and crossing over the original arc. Continue the new arc to meet the horizontal line, again at a right angle, about 0.75 cm (⁵/₁₆ in.) in from the original

arc. It is necessary only to draw the curve on one quarter, as the pattern can be folded up before cutting out; this will ensure it is symmetrical. The beginning and end of the curve must be at right angles where they meet the straight lines, otherwise the tip will either have a slightly pointed effect or will have indentations at these four points. It is also very important to check that the measurement remains the same for the new arc as for the original.

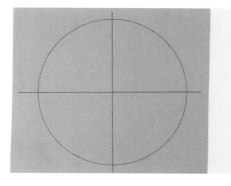

1

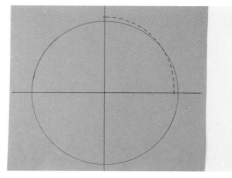

2

3. Once you are happy with the shape and the measurement, add 1 cm (³/₈ in.) seam allowance to the new line. Here, the pattern has been folded, pinned together and cut out, including notches for CF, CB and side points.

Note: It might be necessary to remake the tip if you are not happy with the shape of the oval – it may be too square, or too long, or even too round! In this case, make sure that the measurement doesn't alter when redrawing the curve.

3

4. The finished flared sideband and oval tip.

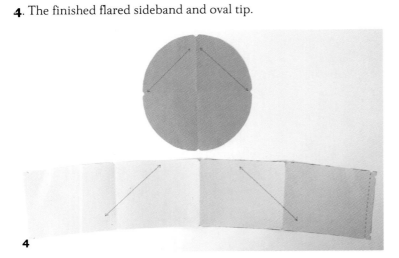

4

3. six-section cap with peak

CROWN

This pattern starts life as a simple rectangle folded in half. The starting point is the same for this large cap in corduroy, on page 45, as for a classic baseball cap. The width of the rectangle should be one-sixth of the head size. The height of the rectangle here is 22 cm ($8^5/_8$ in.), which gives a little extra volume, although 20 cm (8 in.) is a more usual depth for baseball caps and more fitted caps.

1. A piece of A4 paper is large enough for this pattern. Fold in half lengthways, then make two marks on the folded edge 22 cm ($8^5/_8$ in.) apart, for the height. Using a set square to ensure right angles, square out from each mark 4.75 cm ($1^7/_8$ in.) – this is half of the width for one section. This is based on a head size of 57 cm ($22^1/_4$ in.) (57 ÷ 6 = 9.5). Then join up to complete the rectangle, making sure that the new vertical line is also 22 cm ($8^5/_8$ in.).

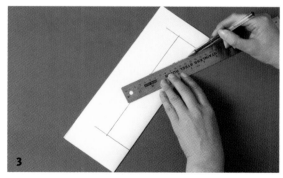

2. The pointed top part of the section should now be drawn. The six sections in this cap join together on the top of the crown in a circle. As there are 360° in a circle, this should be divided by six, to give the correct size of angle for each section. So each section should have an angle of 60° at its top. If this were an eight-section cap, then the angle would be 45° (360 ÷ 8 = 45). Place a protractor over the pattern, so that the centre spot is directly over the top-right corner of the rectangle, on the folded edge. Make sure that the lines of the protractor line up with the lines of the rectangle. Make a pencil mark on the paper at the 60° line on the protractor – this should be 60° from the top horizontal line, but only 30° from the folded edge. (When the pattern is opened out, this will of course give an angle of 60° here.)

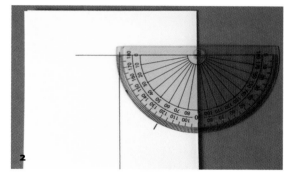

3. Remove the protractor, and draw a line from the top-right corner, going through the mark just made and continuing until the vertical line is crossed.

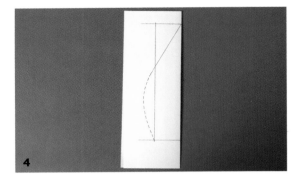

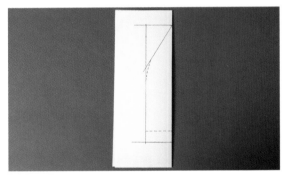

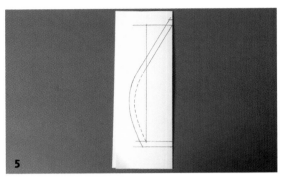

4. Continue this line, curving out slightly and then downwards, to about 2 cm ($^3/_4$ in.) at its widest point before curving in again to meet the bottom-left corner. It is important not to add anything at the bottom edge, as this is the head-fitting line.

5. 1 cm ($^3/_4$ in.) seam allowance is added.

ABOVE An alternative to the wide corduroy cap would be a classic baseball cap, as seen on page 49. In this case, the corner would simply be curved slightly to remove the hard corner effect. This gentle curve will still give quite a square effect when made in fabric.

PEAK

1. Take another A4 piece of paper (this time don't fold). Place the head-fitting template, band or block over the top-right corner of the paper – the CF should sit exactly on the right-hand edge, and the side point of the head fitting should sit exactly on the top edge of the paper. CF is marked along the right-hand edge. Draw in this head-fitting line.

2. Measure 7 cm ($2^3/_4$ in.) down from the CF of the head-fitting line (this is a fairly average size, though it could vary a little) and mark this on the right-hand edge of the paper. Then square across some distance. Now square down from the side point of the head fitting on the top edge of the paper, taking this line down to meet the first at a right angle.

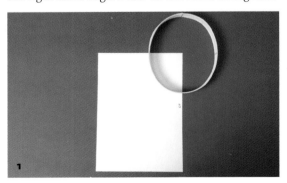

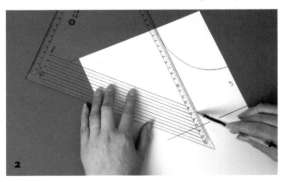

3. Now draw in a curved line, starting at the top and coming out about 1 cm (³/₈ in.) at the side, then curving in across the corner, and curving out again to about 0.5 cm (about ¹/₄ in.), finishing at a right angle to the CF line on the right-hand edge of the paper.

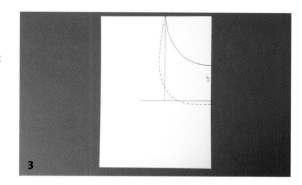

4. This is now looking like a peak, but at the moment this would stick out from the head at a right angle. Cut out this shape and then slash into it from the outside edge towards the head-fitting line, stopping just before reaching it. There should be six slashes, about 2 cm (³/₄ in.) apart at the outside, but narrowing in towards the head fitting.

5. Each slash should be overlapped by 0.5 cm (¹/₄ in.) and taped in place. This will have the effect of stretching the head-fitting line. When placed to fit against the forehead, the peak will now slope downwards gently.

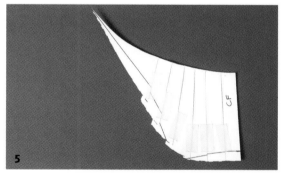

6. Take a fresh piece of A4 paper and fold in half widthways. Pin the pattern onto the new paper, with the CF sitting along the folded edge. Because the peak has become distorted, draw in a new curved line, following the shape but giving it a cleaner line (shown here as a blue broken line).

BELOW An alternative shape is shown here: this is more masculine and is a little shorter, with a slightly square effect. This is the shape of the peak for the cotton shirting cap, seen on page 121.

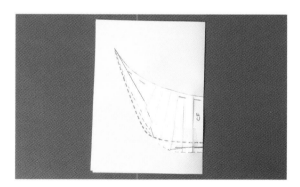

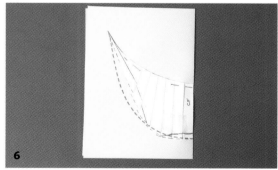

7. The peak has seam allowance added to both edges before being cut out and opened. Both patterns are shown here complete.

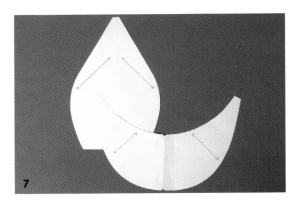

7

This six-section cap by Stephen Jones is made from a textured viscose, and has a contrasting stitched leather wide peak and button. PHOTO: PETER ASHWORTH

4. simple beret

1. The radius for this circular beret is 15 cm (6 in.) and is a little too large for a standard compass set. Instead, fold the paper into quarters. Measure out from the corner 15 cm (6 in.) to form an arc which will be one quarter of the circumference.

2. Repeat the process for the sideband, this time with a slightly smaller radius of 14.5 cm (5³/₄ in.). This is in contrast to most crowns, where the sideband is slightly larger than the tip and must be eased on, giving quite a definite edge. Here, as rounded an effect as possible is required, so the tip here will be eased onto the sideband.

3. The sideband must have a head-fitting cut out at the centre: use the template to draw in a head-fitting line. Make sure that the CF or CB and one side point line up exactly on the folded edges of the paper.

4. Measure 1 cm (³/₈ in.) inside of the head-fitting line to give a seam allowance here.

5. Both pattern pieces can now be cut out and notches snipped for CF, CB and two side points. Pin the layers together first each time to stop them moving while cutting.

6. The completed pattern pieces.

1

3
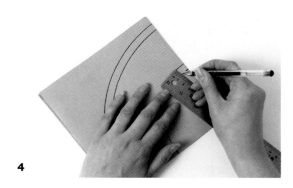

4
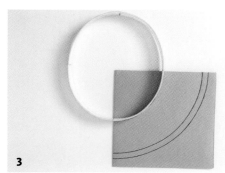

6
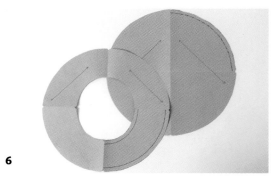

5. simple visor

This is a simple flat visor that slopes down from the top of the head, rather than protruding from the forehead, and will be kept in place on the head with an elastic.

1. Fold a piece of paper in half, and label the folded edge as CF. Like the peak, this starts as a rectangle: the top edge measures 17 cm (6³/₄ in.) (this is half the measurement from ear to ear, going over the top of the head, just as with a wired headband – see page 32). The vertical line measures the required length of the visor – in this case it is 18 cm (7¹/₈ in.).

2. The broken line has been drawn freehand. The first part at the top will be the pointed part of the visor that fits behind the ear at each side.

3. Pin the layers together before cutting out. Then open the pattern out and label it. This doesn't have seam allowance, as the straw will be wired and bound on each edge.

1

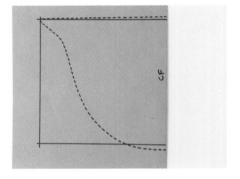

2

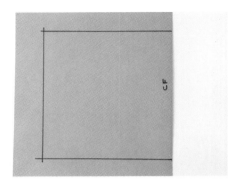

ABOVE The trilby here mixes the two disciplines of handmade millinery with cut and sewn hat-making techniques. The soft velour felt crown has been blocked over a traditional trilby block, while the wool/cashmere brim has been made from a flat pattern and machine-stitched together.

ABOVE RIGHT This parasisal visor is cut from a pattern in the same way as for the panama visor, although here the shape is slightly asymmetric, and the edges are rolled. From the Windswept Collection®.

RIGHT The classic beret seen in a deep-red suede.

This perching hat has been made from a blocked sinamay brim that has been cut into sections and arranged together, finished with scattered crystals to catch the light. From Up Up & Away couture collection.

glossary

Bias The diagonal part of a woven fabric with a lot of stretch

Bind A fabric or ribbon edge on a brim

Block (*noun*) a three-dimensional form, usually made of wood, on which raw materials are shaped to create hats
(*verb*) shaping raw materials on a three-dimensional form

Buckram A very firm cotton canvas with glue embedded. Used as a base for fabric hats, or components of hats

Brim The lower part of a hat, protruding from the head at an angle

Capeline A type of hood (felt or straw) with quite a small crown (top) section, but a large brim, used for medium to large brimmed hats

CB Abbreviation for the centre-back of a hat

CF Abbreviation for the centre-front of a hat

Collar A detachable part of a brim block, for blocking a head-fitting

Cone A bell-shaped hood (felt or straw) with a larger surface area at the crown part but no brim, used for larger crowns, also small-brimmed or brimless hats

Crown The upper part of a hat, covering the head

Cut-and-sewn Refers to fabric hats that have been made from flat patterns and machine-stitched

Domette A soft cotton interlining with a slightly raised surface, available as fusible or sew-in

Fusible Refers to fabric (usually interlining) that can be ironed onto another fabric

Hatter Hat-maker, specifically of men's traditional hats

Head-fitting The inside part of a hat that fits around the head. Also refers to a petersham ribbon cut to a head-size

Hood Unfinished basic hat shape (felt or straw) available as either a capeline or cone shape

Milliner/millinery The art and trade of ladies hats. The origin of the word is Milaners, dating from the 17th century, referring to tradesmen from that city who arrived in the UK to sell hat-making materials and trimmings and later settled

Model millinery Couture hats that have been entirely handmade by an individual milliner

Parasisal Fine straw from the sisal plant; para, sometimes spelt 'pari', refers to a herringbone-type weave

Peak The part of a cap protruding from the forehead

Petersham ribbon A ridged ribbon made of cotton/viscose

Pressing pad Soft cotton fabric formed into a small cushion. Used when ironing small, rounded shapes

Selvedge The finished edge on fabric, running down each side. Also found on the outside edge of woven straw hoods

Sideband In a two-part crown, this refers to the lower section which wraps around the head

Sinamay Woven straw fabric from the abaca (banana) plant, sold by the metre. Mostly made in the Philippines

Staflex A type of fusible cotton fabric

Tarlatan A muslin-type cotton fabric with glue/starch added to give a firm but very light finish. Can be used as a sew-in interlining for soft hats, or cut into bias strips to cover a wired edge

Tip In a two-part crown, this is the topmost section, sits on top of the head

Trimming (*noun*) the decorative features attached to a hat or headpiece

Visor Another word for peak. Often used to describe a stand-alone peak, not attached to a cap

A sculpted perching cap made from a very fine vintage parasisal straw, from Up Up & Away couture collection.

list of suppliers

UK

Baxter Hart & Abraham Ltd
141 New Bedford Road
Luton LU3 1LF
hornbha@aol.com
www.baxterhart.co.uk

Boon & Lane Ltd
7–11 Taylor Street
Luton LU2 0EY
www.blockmaker.com

Ellie Rose Ltd
Unit 8 The Centre
Lakes Industrial Park
Braintree CM7 3RU
Ellie-rose@btconnect.com
www.ellie-rose.com

F. Ruegger Ltd
The Block House
24–26 Clarendon Road
Luton LU2 7PQ
www.ruegger.co.uk

Guy Morse-Brown
Mill Lane Farmhouse
Mill Lane
Wombourne WV5 0LE
www.hatblocks.co.uk

Jaffe et Fils Ltd
The Old Brushworks
Castle Hill
Axminster EX13 5PY
www.jaffefeathers.co.uk

MacCulloch & Wallis
25 Dering Street
London W1S 1AT

macculloch@psilink.co.uk
www.macculloch-wallis.co.uk

Millfields
Solbys Lane
Hadleigh
Benfleet SS7 2NG
www.flowermakers.co.uk

Milliner Warehouse
35 Ebury Bridge Road
London SW1W 8QX
info@millinerwarehouse.com
www.millinerwarehouse.com

Morplan (for fashion
    workroom supplies)
56 Great Titchfield Street
London W1W 7DF
www.morplan.com

Parkin Fabrics Ltd
Prince of Wales Business Park
Vulcan Street
Oldham OL1 4ER
info@parkin-fabrics.co.uk
www.parkin-fabrics.co.uk

Randall Ribbons
12 Frederick Street
Luton LU2 7QS
sales@randallribbons.co.uk
www.randallribbons.co.uk

The Trimming Company
Woburn House
1 Duke Street
Luton LU2 0HJ
sales@thetrimmingcompany.com
www.thetrimmingcompany.com

Trade journal:
The Hat Magazine
170 Brick Lane
London E1 6RU
info@thehatmagazine.com
www.thehatmagazine.com

Useful websites:
www.britishhatguild.co.uk

FRANCE
Artnuptia
32 rue Notre-Dame des
    Victoires
75002 Paris
artnuptia@wanadoo.fr
www.artnuptia.free.fr

GERMANY
Wolfram Kopka
Am Rankewerk 2–4
D-50321 Bruehl
info@kopka.de
www.kopka.de

HOLLAND
Van der Broek
Stationsstraat 52
NL-6365 CK Schinnen
info@hoedenmallen.nl
www.hoedenmallen.nl

Hoedendingen
Kerkstraat 31
NL-6988 AE Lathum
hoedendingen@planet.nl
www.hoedendingen.nl

ITALY
Fratelli Reali
Via Pierluigi da Palestrina,
    31–33
50144 Firenze
info@fratellireali.it
www.fratellireali.it

USA
Hats by Leko
PO Box 170
Odell
OR 97044
info@hatsupply.com
www.hatsupply.com

Jay Gerish Co
2 York Avenue
West Caldwell
NJ 07006
info@jaygerish.com
www.jaygerish.com

Judith M
104 S. Detroit St
LaGrange
IN 46761
info@judithm.com
www.judithm.com

AUSTRALIA
Cyril J. Preston
38 Walsh Street
West Melbourne 3003
Victoria
simon@cjpreston.com.au
www.cjpreston.com.au

De Lew Designs
15 Crisp Drive
Wagga Wagga
NSW 2650
Dlew8323@bigpond.net.au
www.delew.com.au

Melbourne Hat Blocks
Unit 3
2 Celia Street
Bentleigh East
Victoria 3165
www.melbournehatblocks.com.au

Useful websites:
www.makinghats.com.au
www.millineryaustralia.org

further reading

BOOKS ON HATS

Hats – Status, Style and Glamour, Colin McDowell, Thames &
    Hudson, 1992.
The Hat: Trends and Traditions, Madeleine Ginsburg, Studio
    Editions Ltd, 1990.
The Century of Hats, Susie Hopkins, Quintet, 1999.

index

make

hats